# AMERICAN IDOL AFTER IRAQ

### Competing for Hearts and Minds in the Global Media Age

Nathan Gardels

Mike Medavoy

D1509552

WILEY-BLACKWELL

A John Wiley & Sons, Ltd., Publication

This edition first published 2009
© 2009 Nathan Gardels and Mike Medavoy

Blackwell Publishing was acquired by John Wiley & Sons in February 2007. Blackwell's publishing program has been merged with Wiley's global Scientific, Technical, and Medical business to form Wiley-Blackwell.

*Registered Office*
John Wiley & Sons Ltd, The Atrium, Southern Gate, Chichester, West Sussex, PO19 8SQ, United Kingdom

*Editorial Offices*
350 Main Street, Malden, MA 02148-5020, USA
9600 Garsington Road, Oxford, OX4 2DQ, UK
The Atrium, Southern Gate, Chichester, West Sussex, PO19 8SQ, UK

For details of our global editorial offices, for customer services, and for information about how to apply for permission to reuse the copyright material in this book please see our website at www.wiley.com/wiley-blackwell.

The right of Nathan Gardels and Mike Medavoy to be identified as the author of this work has been asserted in accordance with the Copyright, Designs and Patents Act 1988.

*Library of Congress Cataloging-in-Publication Data*

Gardels, Nathan.
  American idol after Iraq : competing for hearts and minds in the global media age / Nathan Gardels and Mike Medavoy.
    p. cm.
  Includes bibliographical references and index.
  ISBN 978-1-4051-8742-8 (hardcover : alk. paper) – ISBN 978-1-4051-8741-1 (pbk. : alk. paper)
  1. Motion pictures, American–Foreign countries. 2. Motion pictures, American–Foreign countries–Influence. I. Medavoy, Mike. II. Title.
  PN1993.5.U6G32 2009
  791.430973'090511–dc22

                                                            2008040246

A catalogue record for this book is available from the British Library.

Set in 11/14pt Sabon by SPi Publisher Services, Pondicherry, India
Printed in Singapore by Utopia Press Pte Ltd

001   2009

# Contents

# List of Plates

# Foreword

Though Barack Obama's election has given it a considerable boost, American soft power has declined in recent years. Power is the ability to affect others to obtain the outcomes one wants, and soft power is the ability to do so through attraction rather than coercion or payments.

The resources that produce soft power for a country include its culture (where it is attractive to others); its values (where they are attractive and not undercut by inconsistent practices); and its policies (where they are seen as inclusive and legitimate in the eyes of others). When poll respondents are asked why they report a decline in American soft power, they cite American policies more than American culture or values. Since it is easier for a country to change its policies than its culture, this implies the possibility that America can recover some of its soft power. Under the right circumstances, American culture can still serve as a soft power resource. Nathan Gardels and Mike Medavoy, with their first-hand cultural knowledge, are excellent guides through this world.

Some analysts have drawn analogies between the current struggle against terrorism and the Cold War. Most outbreaks of transnational terrorism in the past century took a generation to burn out. But another aspect of the analogy has been neglected.

Despite numerous errors, Cold War strategy involved a smart combination of hard coercive power and the soft attractive power of ideas. When the Berlin Wall finally collapsed, it was not destroyed by an artillery barrage, but by hammers and bulldozers wielded by those who had lost faith in communism.

There is very little likelihood that the US can ever attract people like Osama bin Laden. Hard power is necessary to deal with such cases. But there is enormous diversity of opinion in the Muslim world. Witness Iran, whose ruling mullahs see American culture as the Great Satan, but where many in the younger generation want American videos to play in the privacy of their homes. Many Muslims disagree with American values as well as policies, but that does not mean they agree with bin Laden. At the strategic level, soft power helps isolate the extremists and deprive them of recruits. Even at the tactical level, soft power tools – giving small gifts, donating supplies to communities, and granting requests for immigration and education – are an important part of our arsenal.

In the information age, success is not merely the result of whose army wins, but also whose story wins. The current struggle against extreme Islamist terrorism is not a clash of civilizations, but a civil war within Islam. The US can not win unless the Muslim mainstream wins. While we need hard power to battle the extremists, we need the soft power of attraction to win the hearts and minds of the majority.

There has not been enough discussion in the US about the role of American soft power, and our political leaders often squander it with inept policies. Soft power is an analytical term not a political slogan, and perhaps that is why, not surprisingly, it has taken hold in academic analysis, and in other places like Europe, China, and India, but not in the American political debate.

Of course soft power is not the solution to all problems. Even though North Korean dictator Kim Jong Il likes to watch Hollywood movies, that is unlikely to affect his nuclear weapons program. And soft power got nowhere in attracting the Taliban government away from its support for Al Qaeda in the 1990s. It took hard military power to end that. But other goals such as the promotion of democracy and human rights are better achieved by soft power. Soft power often takes longer to show effects, but it is often a more effective instrument for accomplishing contextual goals. In addition it can create an enabling or disabling environment for the accomplishment of short term goals as the US discovered in the aftermath of the invasion of Iraq. Skeptics, who belittle soft power because it does not solve all problems, are like a boxer who fights without using his left hand because his right hand is stronger.

Defense Secretary Robert Gates has called for the US government to commit more money and effort to soft power tools including diplomacy, economic assistance, and communications because the military alone cannot defend America's interests around the world. He pointed out that military spending totals nearly half a trillion dollars annually compared with a State Department budget of $36 billion. In his words, "I am here to make the case for strengthening our capacity to use soft power and for better integrating it with hard power."

Military force is obviously a source of hard power, but the same resource can sometimes contribute to soft power behavior. A well run military can be a source of attraction, and military to military cooperation and training programs, for example, can establish transnational networks that enhance a country's soft power. The impressive job of the American military in providing humanitarian relief after the Indian Ocean tsunami and the South Asian earthquake in 2005 helped restore the attractiveness of the United States.

Of course, misuse of military resources can also undercut soft power. The Soviet Union had a great deal of soft power in the years after World War II, but they destroyed it by the way they used their hard power against Hungary and Czechoslovakia. Brutality and indifference to just war principles of discrimination and proportionality can also destroy legitimacy. The efficiency of the initial American military invasion of Iraq in 2003 created admiration in the eyes of some foreigners, but that soft power was undercut by the subsequent inefficiency of the occupation and the scenes of mistreatment of prisoners at Abu Ghraib.

Many of America's soft power resources lie outside of government in the private sector and civil society, in our bilateral alliances, multilateral institutions, and transnational contacts. Many official instruments of soft or attractive power – public diplomacy, broadcasting, exchange programs, development assistance, disaster relief, military to military contacts – are scattered around the government and there is no overarching strategy or budget that even tries to integrate them. We spend about 500 times more on the military than we do on broadcasting and exchanges combined. And how should the government relate to the non-official generators of soft power – everything from Hollywood to Harvard to the Gates Foundation – that emanate from our civil society? The best way to begin to understand these important questions is to read the pages that follow.

Joseph S. Nye Jr.

Professor Joseph S. Nye Jr. teaches at the John F. Kennedy School of Government, Harvard University. He is the author of *Soft Power: The Means to Success in World Politics*.

He has served as Assistant Secretary of Defense for International Security Affairs, Chair of the National Intelligence Council, and Deputy Under Secretary of State for Security Assistance, Science, and Technology.

# Chapter 1

# Hearts, Minds, and Hollywood

The conflicts of the future are going to be as much about the abundant cultural flows of the global information economy as about the scarcity of resources. This is because contending values have been crowded into a common public square created by freer trade, the spread of technology, and the planetary reach of the media.

Only in such a world could a cartoon of the Prophet Mohammed in an obscure Danish daily newspaper inflame the pious and mobilize the militant across the vast and distant stretches of the Islamic world. Only in such a world would bloodied Tibetan monks be censored out of Chinese TV news reports just to show up on YouTube, or would a CNN pundit in New York be sued by a Beijing school teacher for calling Chinese "thugs" and their exports "junk." Only in such a world would the Vatican launch an all out assault on the *Da Vinci Code* movie to convince audiences that popular fiction is not the same as eternal truth.

This global public square is the new space of power where images compete and ideas are contested; it is where hearts and minds are won or lost and legitimacy is established. It is a space both of friction and fusion where the cosmopolitan commons of the twenty-first century is being forged.

Though facing intense challenges, the core of the global information economy today remains America's media-industrial complex, including Hollywood entertainment. If culture is on the front line of world affairs in the times to come, then Hollywood, as much as Silicon Valley, the Pentagon, or the US State Department, has a starring role.

In this book, Hollywood – broadly defined as the commercial and professional production of American popular culture for mass distribution, but focusing on the film industry – is our main prism. The reasons for Hollywood's power over the last 100 years are clear. Long before celluloid or pixels were invented, Plato understood that those who tell the stories also rule. And if music sets the mood for the multitudes, the warblings of Sinatra, Madonna, and Metallica have certainly been the muzak of the American-led world order.

Above all, as philosophers have told us, images – the currency of Hollywood – rule dreams and dreams rule actions. That is because most people construct the worldview which informs what they do more on an emotional than a rational basis. They buy into a narrative not so much through the considered weighing of ideas as on what image they want to be a part of or associated with. What people identify with, or don't, depends on the dignity, recognition, and status those images – "that which presents an intellectual and emotional complex in an instant of time" in the famous words of the poet Ezra Pound – confer in their culture[1]. In short, a person's vision of "the good life" is largely determined by what works for them metaphorically.

It is why Saddam regularly played the Sinatra tune "My Way" at his birthday party and it is why we associate a moment of carefree, dancing joy with "Singin' In the Rain." It is why a middle-aged man buys a Porsche and why a teenager desperately desires a pair of Pumas. Sometimes, the symbol can be more generic, as when blue jeans spread worldwide after the 1960s as a ready-to-wear statement about non-conformity and informal lifestyle. Biographers and fashion editors to this day regularly dredge up Jackie Kennedy, Grace Kelly, Audrey Hepburn, or Elizabeth Taylor when they want to evoke the glamour of a bygone era in an age of Wal Mart aesthetics. When Carla Bruni, a.k.a. Mrs. Sarkozy, showed up for a state visit on the staid shores of Britain, her gray cashmere coatdress and pill box hat immediately evoked Jackie O mixed with the lost glamour of Princess Di in the London press. By far, this impression outweighed in the public eye President Sarkozy's hints about France rejoining NATO.

Tomorrow's style nostalgia may include Leonardo DiCaprio, Brad Pitt, or Julia Roberts, who stand in the place taken by Katherine Hepburn, Marlon Brando or Paul Newman for an earlier generation.

Apprehending the world by what works metaphorically is why the Camorra gang from Sicily mimics Hollywood films in its actual lifestyle, with women bodyguards wearing yellow tracksuits like Uma Thurman in Quentin Tarantino's *Kill Bill*. It is why the villa of one of its top bosses was modeled down to the last detail on the mansion of Tony Montana in Brian De Palma's *Scarface*.[2]

More profoundly, adopting a worldview by what works metaphorically is also why humiliated youths in Gaza, feeling righteous and empowered, cheered Al Qaeda taking down the Twin Towers on 9/11. Its why Mexico's demographic experts credit the daytime soaps with helping reduce the population explosion in that thoroughly Catholic nation.

In international affairs, public opinion doesn't pick apart policies analytically but forms its sensibilities based on images. Where the Statue of Liberty once symbolized America, to many that symbol became the hooded prisoner at Abu Ghraib during the Bush tenure (though the very fact of Barack Obama's election as president did more than all the years of

Bush's public diplomacy to restore some shimmer to America's image). In Japan's case, where once there was Tojo now there is Toyota. In the early post-Cold War days, Gorbachev taking his granddaughter to a McDonald's said one thing. A muscular, bare-chested Putin hunting boar in the Russian bush says something entirely more menacing, closer to a Ramboesque KGB assertion of raw power than the image of glasnost or Swan Lake with which the West felt comfortable.

Lacking direct experience in the reality of others, such images are known largely through the media. The biggest projector of images in human history, of course, has been Hollywood. By and large, what Americans know about the world, and what the world knows about America, they know from the screen. Of the 20 percent of Americans who own passports, less than 10 percent travel abroad in any given year,[3] a situation bound to get worse with the falling dollar. And, in 2008, American film exports were 10 times larger than film imports, a balance of trade more favorable than any other industry but aerospace.[4]

Often what foreign audiences learn is incidental – the well-appointed kitchen in the *Leave it to Beaver* TV show, the two cars in the driveway or kids with their own bedroom in such thrillers as *When a Stranger Calls* (an unimaginable amount of private space in most places in the world), the expectation of fair treatment under the law and the sincerity of weighing fairness and justice in *Twelve Angry Men*, the casual relationship between boys and girls as the backdrop to shows like *Friends*, or even the most innocent Disney Channel shows like *Hannah Montana*. Sometimes films and television shows mislead outsiders about American life, for example by the near total absence of religious expression in mainstream entertainment, leaving impressions, like the shadows in Plato's cave, far from the truth. This "second order" communication is often as powerful in the perception of the viewer as the first-order dramatic plot.

Osama bin Laden has never been the United States; he only watched it on TV when he was growing up in Saudi Arabia. Most of the nouveau riche Chinese who buy up the California-style tract houses in suburban Beijing have never been to the Orange County their development replicates; they've only watched *The O.C.* on pirated videos or satellite TV. Conversely, and just as significantly, what all too many Americans think they know about the rest of the world comes from movies like *Around the World in 80 Days*, *The Manchurian Candidate*, John Wayne's *The Green Berets*, the *Deer Hunter*, *Mission Impossible III*, the James Bond series, or *The Bourne Identity*.

If there is a genius to Osama bin Laden's madness in this context, it is that he understands that insular Americans, who don't look back and don't look around, also don't think much about the rest of the world unless it intrudes upon their pursuit of happiness in a sensational way. In this vein, Al Qaeda has taken a page from the Hollywood handbook. It's real expertise is not military damage, but media manipulation through sensational acts of special-effects terror that rivet attention – both in the West and across the Muslim *ummah* (community) – in a world crowded with other messages. Also grasping that America is a post-textual society that obtains information mainly from movies, television, or the Net, Osama bin Laden knows it is images, not concepts, that break through. Thus, blockbuster acts of terror are the forte of this virtual caliph.

Unfortunately for the rest of the Muslim *ummah*, such powerful images work the other way as well. For most post-textual Americans, the "people of the Book" – Muslims – are now known mostly through sensational images of terror staged by Al Qaeda and its allies, including the attacks in Mumbai in 2008. The same terrifying images that inspire defiance in the young kid in Gaza also sow the seeds of fear and loathing among westerners.

In the global battle for hearts and minds, America once had the metaphorical upper hand because we dominated the flow of images, icons, and information, not to speak of English being the lingua franca thanks not only to American hegemony but that of the British Empire before it. The democratization of media through technology is making that less true every day.

Where CNN, MGM, and the BBC once ruled, now there are 75 million Chinese blogs,[5] CCTV, Al Jazeera, Al Arabiya, and the Dubai Film Festival, as well as 200 satellite channels across the Arab world. A proliferation of jihadist websites, which have joined benign telemuslims like Egypt's Amr Khaled in competing for the Arab soul, are every bit as influential as YouTube or Facebook in their own demographic. Without doubt, the Internet is the single most empowering tool for recruitment and networking of jihadists. Where once American soap operas like *Days of Our Lives* filled boob tubes globally, now Brazilian, Mexican, or Korean daytime TV have as great or even greater appeal. Though for the moment Hollywood may still command the shock and awe blockbuster, national cinemas, as has long been the case in India, are gaining traction even as Hollywood itself is showing signs, if so far meager, of taking on a more cosmopolitan cast.

In the midst of this technological and cultural democratization, America's once lustrous image has become tarnished by the misadventure in Iraq, Guantanamo and the Bush White House defense of torture, not to speak of the globally broadcast scenes of the Katrina catastrophe, the Britney breakdown, Wall St. corruption and the mortgage crash brought on by too much consumption and too little financial regulation (generating not a little schadenfreude among those we scolded in the Asian crisis a little more than a decade ago). It also doesn't help that while the US has 5 percent of the world's population, it has 25 percent of the world's incarcerated.[6]

Despite America's considerable technological and higher-educational prowess, we can, therefore, no longer assume, as we did in the triumphant days after the end of the Cold War, that global public opinion will buy into the American narrative. We can no longer assume that the world out there so readily identifies with our idea of "the good life" as universally appealing. In what amounts to a global glasshouse of instantaneous information with planetary reach, we must contend for hearts and minds just like everyone else. The images of those bloodied Tibetan monks, censored within China, competed for sympathy in global public opinion with those of the Paralympics torchbearer, Jin Jing, who struggled from her wheelchair to protect the Olympic torch from the rough assault by a Tibetan protestor in Paris. Indeed, the Chinese government skillfully sought to recast its image through leveraging the world media's coverage of the 2008 Olympics. Before he dropped out in protest over Chinese inaction on genocide in Darfur, the authorities had recruited Steven Spielberg for this purpose. In the end another director, Zhang Yimou, masterfully orchestrated the Olympic ceremonies. That is indicative of what is to come with the rise of the rest in what Fareed Zakaria has called "the Post-American World."

This book is about grappling with this challenge, so to speak, of *American Idol* after Iraq. It is about understanding the power of the image, the rise of that power manifested by the global dominance of American entertainment culture and the reaction to it. It is about the increasing dispersion of that power due to globalization. And it is about grabbing hold of the power of the image as a tool of cultural diplomacy in America's quest to restore its lost luster.

## Notes

1. Kermode, F. (2008) "Ezra Conquers London." *New York Review of Books*, vol. 55, no. 22.

2. Stille, A. (2008) "Italy: The Crooks in Control." *New York Review of Books*, vol. 55, no. 6.
3. http://www.gyford.com/phil/writing/2003/01/31/how_many_america. php. Also: tinet.ita.do.gov/cat/f-2006-101-002html.
4. Bayles, M. "Risky Business for Hollywood." *International Herald Tribune*, May 8, 2008.
5. Kristof, N. D. "Earthquake and Hope." *New York Times*, May 26, 2008.
6. Liptak, A. "Inmate Count in US Dwarfs Other Nations'." *New York Times*, April 23, 2008. http://www.nytimes.com/2008/04/23/us/23prison. html?_r=.

# Chapter 2

# The Magic is Gone – Except at the Box Office

During the presidential primaries, Barack Obama disparagingly noted that U.S. senators scoping out the international scene often see "the desperate faces" in places like Darfur or Baghdad from the height of a helicopter. "It makes you stop and wonder," he mused, "when those faces look up at an American helicopter, do they feel hope, or do they feel hate?"[1]

More than an empathetic insight, this question of how the world sees America is paramount today since our image has never been so damaged as during the George W. Bush reign. A BBC World Service poll in 2007 of people across 25 countries revealed that one in two believe the United States has been playing a mainly negative role in the world.[2] The most reliable polling by the Pew Foundation further documents a sobering reality: In Turkey, a presumed ally in a key region, only 9% have a favorable view of the US. In Pakistan, a supposed key partner in the war on terror, it is 16% and worsening. The favorable view of America by Germans dropped from 60% to 30% between 2002 to 2007.[3] According to the Pew pollsters, these numbers improved slightly in 2008 – but only in anticipation of President Bush's departure from power.

In the popular play *Black Watch* about the Scottish regiment serving in the "coalition of the willing" in Iraq along with the US, one disillusioned soldier dropped the rhetoric about spreading democracy to bitterly quip that "porn and petrol" was the Western way of life he was there, risking his life and killing others, to promote and protect.

No doubt, as *Foreign Policy* editor Moisés Naim has argued, much of this anti-American sentiment is a disguised yearning for the familiar American leadership of the post-World War II era, still considered indispensable in a world lurching from an old order to a new one.

Certainly, a Barack Obama presidency will go a long way in quelling the broad contempt out there, at least in Europe, the Middle East, Africa, and Latin America. East Asia, which, overall, tends to pay more attention to interests than values, seems less enamored with Obama and more concerned about protectionism. John K. Glenn, the foreign policy director of the German Marshall Fund, told the *Washington Post* in June, 2008 that Obama "reaffirms in European minds the vitality of the U.S."[4] Dominique Moïsi, one of France's most prominent foreign policy analysts, was absolutely gushing when he told the *Financial Times* that same June that "America, thanks to Obama, has returned to be the emotional center of gravity of the world."[5] Famously, a Hamas spokesman said he preferred Obama as president.

Nonetheless, anyone who thinks a trust has not been broken between America and the world is also not reading the figures right. The new US president clearly has his work cut out for him.

The challenge of bringing America back is great indeed since our famed beacon has dimmed. Our prestige was at such at an all-time high when the Berlin Wall fell in 1989 that the neo-conservative intellectual Francis Fukuyama confidently proclaimed we had arrived at the "end of history," which amounted to the rest of the world becoming more like us. By 2007 Joyce Carol Oates, writing in the *Atlantic*,[6] was compelled to admit that the rest of the world had come to see "the American idea" as a "cruel joke." "How heartily sick the world has grown, in the first seven years of the 21st century, of the American idea!" she wrote.

The assessment of Brent Scowcroft, who helped George H. W. Bush end the Cold War with a whimper instead of bang, is characteristically straightforward. "We are losing our aura of 'specialness,' the belief that the US is a different sort of great power from the others," the supreme realist of American foreign policy has said. "As a result, people are increasingly unwilling to give us and our policies the benefit of the doubt. We are increasingly treated the same as any other wholly self-interested power."[7]

Shirin Ebadi, the Iranian lawyer and Nobel peace laureate, confirmed Scowcrofts's worst fears. "America was once recognized as the standard of human rights everywhere. But I see these pictures of Abu Ghraib and Iraq and ask myself 'What happened to American civilization?'" In an interview she recounted how, during all her dark years struggling against the ayatollahs for human rights, Eleanor Roosevelt and the UN Human Rights Charter she helped draft were her inspiration. "Of all the apologies in order by America's leaders," Ebadi said, "one of the most important is an apology to the spirit of Mrs. Roosevelt."[8]

Bernard Kouchner, the most pro-American French foreign minister in memory, simply offered this cutting geocultural epitaph for America in early 2008: "The magic is gone."[9]

Even Karen Hughes, George Bush's Texas confidante who tried fruitlessly to boost America's image through public diplomacy, said on leaving her job in 2007 that it would take "decades" to overcome the intense hostility around the world toward the US. It would be, she said, "a long struggle."[10] If politics in the information age is about whose story wins, America has certainly been on a losing streak.

Yet, even as America's official reputation has tanked, Hollywood – to use the catch-all phrase for American mass culture – has enjoyed unprecedented success abroad. In 2008, US films earned $17 billion at the foreign box office compared to $9.6 billion at home.[11]

International ticket sales for Hollywood films now account for 60% of overall box office receipts, up from 40% in 2005. *Spider-Man 3* was the biggest worldwide opener in history, bringing in $375 million. *The Simpsons Movie* grossed nearly $333 million abroad, twice what it made in the US. All during the years of post-invasion disaster in Iraq, shock and awe blockbusters from Hollywood remained popular around the world. In the 2007 Pew poll, 60% of Lebanese described Americans as greedy, violent, and immoral, yet Lebanon is one of Hollywood's hottest markets in the Middle East.[12] According to Martha Bayles, the most popular shows on Arab satellite TV were *Sex and the City*, *South Park*, *Friends*, *Seinfeld*, and *Oprah*.[13]

This builds upon a strong trend since the late 1980s. As the Yale Center for the Study of Globalization reports, between 1986 and 2000 American entertainment exports increased 426% from a volume of $1.68 billion to $8.85 billion.[14]

To the extent pirating is the sincerest form of mass cultural flattery, it is surely a statement that even in Tehran, where we've been locked in combat with the country's leadership over their nuclear program, you can find purloined copies of *Rugrats Go Wild* or *The Incredibles* sold on the street for less than two dollars.

In China today, where freedom of speech is restricted, the Internet is widely used as the conduit to distribute pirated films, television shows such as *24*, *Desperate Housewives*, and *CSI* or *Friends*.[15] Bored by their own restrained media and doubtful of official information, affluent Chinese youth gorge on American music, movies, and TV shows. It is perhaps a way of creating a parallel, detached reality for them and their circle of friends even if it follows the script of apolitical consumerism that cements Communist Party power.

This wild discrepancy between political polling about America's image and box-office receipts or rampant pirating suggests that America's mass cultural presence has transcended our formal foreign policy institutions.

Clearly, then, any strategy aimed at rebuilding America's image must go beyond the usual analysis and prescriptions of foreign policy professionals and acknowledge that America's impact in the world has as much to do with what emanates from outside of Washington as inside the Beltway.

Unlike most countries, America's image is based not only on who we are and what we do, but on how we present ourselves to the world through our globally pervasive mass culture – Hollywood films, popular music, YouTube videos, and TV. No empire in history – not the Romans, not the British, the Spanish, nor the Ottomans – has possessed the world-straddling, image-molding capacity to project its way of life to others quite like our powerful media-industrial complex.

As a result, what we are, what we do, and how we present ourselves, incidentally or purposefully, are inextricably meshed in the minds-eye of global public opinion. As importantly, our own collective self-image vis-à-vis the rest of the world is shaped by how we present ourselves in the media. Movies, whether *Apocalypse Now* or *The Simpsons*, are at once a reflection of the American experience and a shaper of it.

As much as the foreign policy analysts of the Connecticut Avenue think tanks might believe otherwise, it is all of a piece. The collage of images flows out in no particular order, the good and the bad, direct political communication as well as the "second order" impact of TV, movies, and music, all thrown into the blender of perception. Both contribute to the rational and emotional construction of what people believe to be the American reality. Guantanamo. Abu Ghraib. Obama. *The Simpsons.* Blackwater. MIT. Bling. Harvard. Microsoft. Google. Britney. Katrina. *Family Guy.* Arnold Schwarzenegger. Hip hop. The Latin Grammys. Obesity. Jay-Z. McDonald's. The Hummer. Sprawl. Preemptive war. Donald Trump. *Desperate Housewives. Oprah. Sex in the City. Mission Impossible III. Titanic. Jurassic Park.* The weak dollar. High-returning hedge funds. Foreclosed homes. The Foo Fighters. *Gone With the Wind. To Kill A Mockingbird.* Paris Hilton. Marlon Brando. Clint Eastwood. *The Bourne Identity.* Bond. George Bush. Bill Clinton. *The Survivor. Lost. American Idol.*

The key issue, of course, is how this all gets sorted out. In part, increasing box-office receipts abroad are due to freer trade and the falling dollar. But clearly, as has long been the case, Hollywood offers a window into America's attractive dynamism as an open-minded and technologically innovative culture, always on the move, discovering the next new thing, "the fun culture" which has largely shed the overbearing strictures of Calvinism, Islam, or Confucianism, albeit with all the decadence of *Girls Gone Wild* excesses thrown in (not to speak of the immense media underworld of web pornography).

Of course, the most attractive attribute in our arsenal of soft power is the image of America as the promised land of infinite possibility and opportunity, where personal liberty reigns and the rule of law is reliable. The America which appeals most deeply to the world is a geocultural therapy for "history's wounded masses." When immigrants get off the boat, they leave their troubles behind. The soil – ancestral territory and all its baggage – is taken out of the soul and becomes the real estate of the free. In this sense, America is more a creed than a race or even a nation. The future, not the past, occupies everyone's imagination. The Nobel poet Octavio Paz called America in this respect, "the Republic of the future."

Surely, this is one of the open secrets of why Muslim immigrants can more easily integrate into the American mainstream and freely practice their faith while, in Europe, they remain linked to the historical tribulations of their homelands.

Though social mobility is clogging up with the greatest class inequality since 1929 – while Mexican immigration of an unprecedented order and fear of terrorism have cramped the embrace of once open arms – America still remains the premier destination of hope to huddled masses who risk their lives to get here across scorching deserts or in the holds of rusty cargo ships. Though bling and celebrity mania may blight the American scene these days, at heart we are not about shameless materialism or hollow fame, but about the dignity and recognition of every individual as worthy enough to get a fair chance in life. This has made America a profoundly aspirational culture, where winning, not just getting by, is part of the game. All of this comes across in cinema from futurist fables like *I Am Legend* with Will Smith to classic Westerns such as the TV series *Gunsmoke* to more contemporary shows like *Friends*.

It would nonetheless be a mistake to see popular ticket sales and prolific pirating of films that portray this life as synonymous with pro-Americanism. Hollywood films may well entertain, amuse, lift people out of their own circumstances, and let them imagine another world, but that doesn't at all mean they embrace the world they see on the screen. Often, and more often lately since 9/11, it can have just the opposite consequence.

The fact that *Mission Impossible III* sold out in movie houses from Tokyo to Cairo even as George Bush was seen as a comparable danger to world peace as Mahmoud Ahmadinejad doesn't mean "the appeal of Hollywood" is an unalloyed asset that only plays a positive role "in inspiring the dreams and desires of others." The reality is more complex. It is often closer to a double-edged sword.

As much as America is a dream to some, it is a target of enmity to others. What some admire others abhor as the home of hubris, arrogance, and decadence. The City on the Hill is seen by some as the very residence of evil, "The Great Satan."

Though the soul of America is a kind of religio-secular hybrid, as the theologian Martin Marty calls it, the materialistic, sexually immodest, and impious messages that pervade our mass media are widely seen by culturally conservative Muslims, not unlike our own homegrown religious conservatives, as lapping at the shores of their faith and identity. Few act as terrorists, of course, but there is a large hinterland of the global Muslim *ummah* that regards the anything-goes-if-it–expands-market-share ethos of ubiquitous American entertainment as a threat to their spiritual survival.

"To study the anti-American critique mounted by radical Islam," the cultural critic Martha Bayles has insightfully noted, "is to see oneself in the equivalent of a fun-house mirror: The reflection is at once both distorted and weirdly accurate.... Our enemies do not question our economic and technological superiority, but they do question our moral and spiritual superiority."[16] In a similar vein, Reuel Marc Gerecht, a former CIA operative in the Middle East, warns against "mirror-imaging the mullahs," by which he means secular analysts dismissing the Islamist critiques of American culture as cynical politics instead of based in belief.[17]

Indeed, well before 9/11, Joe Duffy, who headed the US Information Agency during Bill Clinton's presidency, doubted aloud whether "Hollywood's insistent portrayal of sex, crime and violence which persistently exposes viewers to images and messages that undermine the character of the audience best serves America's broader interests, and ultimately democracy itself."[18] So much programming of this kind, worried this public servant officially responsible for America's image abroad, "only confirms the worst suspicions that the West, and America in particular, is morally corrupt and intellectually devoid." American filmmakers, of course, stand on their constitutional right to free expression in response to such criticism from government.

Though Francis Fukuyama has called for demilitarizing the war on terrorism through the use of more "soft power" – defined by Harvard's Joe Nye as the attractive and persuasive qualities of America as distinct from "hard power" military might – he understands this conundrum. To Fukuyama, America's biggest soft power weapon, Hollywood, often plays a negative role. "It is perceived as the purveyor of the kind of secular, materialistic, permissive culture that is not very popular in many parts of the world, especially the Muslim world."[19] Nye himself argues that American mass culture is a resource. It is only power to the extent it is positively attractive; it loses its power when it reflects a negative image of America.

In our bewilderment after 9/11 many felt that America was attacked because it wasn't understood. But America was definitely understood. The propaganda of postmodern America – the promotion of consumer materialism accompanied by a globalizing relativism of values – had already been out there a long time. Well before the preemptive invasion of Iraq, MTV had already gone where the CIA could never penetrate.

Sumner Redstone, whose Viacom company owns MTV, unwittingly encapsulated the whole issue when he argued at the Nielsen Money & Media Conference in New York at the end of 2007 that, whatever the ultimate evolution of the upheaval in digital distribution which has produced an array of platforms from laptops to cell phone screens, "content was still king." Crowing about Viacom's prowess at making money in this new environment he lauded his secret "content" weapon: "Thanks Britney," he told the media executives gathered before the guru to parse some wisdom about how to get rich as the technological sands keep shifting.

In a Gallup Poll of 8,000 Muslim women in 2006, the overwhelming majority cited "attachment to spiritual and moral values" as the best aspect of their own societies while the most common answer to the question about what they admired least in the West was "moral decay, promiscuity and pornography" the pollsters called "the Hollywood image."[20] A standard line of Jordan's Queen Rania as she tries to bridge the gap between Islam and the West is that many Muslim women see their American counterparts "as desperate housewives seeking sex in the city."[21]

Many in America would agree that not all the fruits of freedom are sublime. From moms like Tipper Gore to comedian Bill Cosby to the Christian right, many Americans also recoil at the content of some American films, popular music, and television as an affront, if not an outright threat, to their traditional values. Karl Rove understood that a reliable foil for the "faith gap" wedge of voters that put George Bush in power the second time around was "liberal Hollywood."

In this context, it is instructive to recall that the whole self-regulatory rating system for films and TV was created precisely in order to prevent censorious political action by conservative groups. Indeed, the Motion Picture Association was founded in 1922 in reaction to a 1915 Supreme Court decision that defined cinema as "business, pure and simple," and therefore not eligible for First Amendment protection. "Because this ruling raised the specter of state censorship, the major film studios agreed," as Martha Bayles has pointed out," to adopt the Production Code that restricted sex and violence. Only later did the courts redefine cinema as protected speech – which is to say, as artistic expression."[22]

There are other weighty voices as well who are less than enthusiastic about America's entertainment culture. Viewing us through the lens of our entertainment media, Pope Benedict XVI has preached warily that America, and the consumerist globalization it fosters, is all about "ego" and "desire." In his 2004 dialogue with Italian senator Marcello Pera, the conservative pontiff worried that while America had "an obvious spiritual foundation," it was being eroded at an "accelerated pace" by the media. "Americans watch too much TV," the former head of the Congregation of the Doctrine of the Faith told his Italian interlocutor.[23] Before him, John Paul II also worried that America had strayed far from truth into an "anything goes" amoral cornucopia of corrosive relativism reflected widely in its globally influential media.

As much as the foreign box office take might suggest otherwise, this occupation of the global imagination by American entertainment has become too overwhelming even for some of those more closely aligned with Hollywood's secular liberal values, stirring a backlash. As Josef Joffe, the publisher of the German weekly *Die Zeit*, has put it: "Between Vietnam and Iraq, America's cultural presence has expanded into ubiquity, and so has resentment of America. Soft power does not necessarily increase the world's love for America. It is still power, and it still makes enemies."[24]

The flipside of this backlash is the robust cultural competition that is part and parcel of the growing civilizational confidence that comes along with the new-found prosperity globalization has wrought, notably in Asia. Increasingly, audiences want to be entertained more by their own myths and stories, soaps and epics, as they have for so long in India, not just by those produced in America. The route to the East, so to speak, may well have gone through the West, but as the East arrives at its destination it increasingly wants the modernity it has glimpsed on the screen on its own terms, not

American terms, and certainly not with our geopolitical, geoeconomic, or geocultural agenda.

The American way experienced through the Hollywood lens may have leavened traditional cultures, particularly those emerging from underdevelopment, but what results is a modernizing hybrid, not a replica replete with the cultural license, consumerism, electoral norms, or other attributes of the "good life" we assume to be universally appealing.

A conversation with any number of Chinese who were educated in American universities but have returned home will reveal they prefer a large dose of order along with their prosperity. Lee Kuan Yew, the godfather of East Asian modernization, is never shy of pointing out that "in China, there is no tradition of satirizing the emperor. To do a Doonesbury cartoon is to commit sedition and treason."[25]

Sitting posture perfect in his resplendent traditional robe, Hamid Karzai will candidly admit the limits on cultural freedom imposed by religious and tribal elders on "the modern state" the US has entrusted him to build in Afghanistan. The elders are angered by "blasphemous" downloads from the Internet or the "immoral" behavior exhibited in Hollywood and Bollywood films alike. (In April 2008 the Minister of Information and Culture, under pressure from the Council of Clerics and supported by Karzai, banned five Indian soap operas, including *Life's Test* and *Because the Mother-in-Law Was Once the Daughter-in Law*, because they "were not in keeping with Afghan religion and culture." The Taliban, of course, had banned television outright.)

In Saudi Arabia, young mainstream men might have pictures of pretty women on their cell phones, downloaded from the Internet, with the theme from *Titanic* as their ringtone, but nonetheless angrily react to running across a woman, albeit covered from head to toe, in a restaurant without her husband. They may watch *Oprah* and *Dr. Phil* on satellite TV while sipping cardamom coffee and smoking in the men's living room at home, but nonetheless support "jihad" against "foreigners" in their "Arab homeland" as a matter of duty and honor.[26] Clearly, double standards are not only the province of the West.

In Turkey, devoted Muslim women are redefining modernity on their own terms. Against Western conceptions, they see wearing the headscarf at the university not only as a sign of piety, but also as a symbol of empowerment and equality with Muslim men. In the Arab world, a plethora of TV sitcoms and talk shows are emerging where the idea is to be "free but conservative," as one Beirut producer put it.

Indeed, we may be witnessing the end of "the end of history" – the making of the world in America's image after the Cold War – and the advent of post-globalization. While globalization flattened the world, now non-American and even non-Western modernity is once again differentiating and diversifying ways of life.

Khan Lee, who runs Zeus studios in Taiwan and is the brother of Ang Lee of *Crouching Tiger, Hidden Dragon* fame, is blunt on this topic: "Hollywood is a dinosaur that has destroyed and occupied our minds for too long. The world is full of new stories waiting to be told and new audiences waiting to see them, even if we use Hollywood's template to do so."[27]

After all, the story of China's richest woman, Zjang Yin of Nine Dragons Paper, who built an empire from scratch recycling cardboard packing crates, is every bit as compelling as the tale of Horatio Alger pulling himself up by his bootstraps.

It can certainly not be a criticism of American hegemony on the wane that we have become less exceptional because the dream of social mobility and opportunity once so unique to America is now more of a reality for others as well. But, because we are less exceptional, of course, it also means

America's own story is relatively less appealing as a model to those with their own version of it.

The irascible Singaporean diplomat, Kishore Mahbubani, makes this critical point in his book, *The New Asian Hemisphere: The Irresistible Shift of Global Power to the East.*[28] "The great paradox about the failed Western attempts to export democracy to other societies," Mahbubani writes, "is that in the broadest sense of the term, the West has actually succeeded in democratizing the world. One key goal of democracy is to empower its citizens to make them believe they are masters of their own destiny. The number of people in the world who believe this has never been higher. Even in the 'undemocratic' society of China, citizens have seized the opportunities provided by the new economic freedoms they enjoy to completely change their lives.... In global terms, there has been a huge democratization of the human spirit. The West should be celebrating this, not berating countries about imperfect voting practices."

For Mahbubani, questions of illiberal democratization aside, the West resists this recognition because it implies a "day of reckoning" is due to arrive in the coming decades when those increasingly in charge of their own destiny will no longer accept the "undemocratic" order where the West is on top.

For all of our might, America is losing its power. As we have noted, our post-Cold War political capital was squandered with unwise unilateralism, the misguided war in Iraq, and the fearful retreat from universal principles in the wake of the 9/11 attacks – damage President Obama can help repair. In part the loss of power is because there is resistance to our overwhelming global presence, not least through our mass culture, and it is in part due to competition from newcomers in what is becoming a truly multipolar world.

For all of these reasons, the John Wayne-era assumption that America could write the script for the whole world, both in Washington and Hollywood, has been foiled forever. Wherever we go from here, it is on new ground.

That new ground where the "long struggle" to burnish America's prestige will take place is in the planetary public square created by the globalizing media.

Like politics, the movies and mass culture that fill this space of power are a communal experience. Arnold Schwarzenegger or Ronald Reagan – or any politician who has gone on the *Daily Show*, *Saturday Night Live*, or Jay Leno's *Tonight Show* to hawk their candidacy – would tell you that, in a democracy, the voting booth and the box office share the same public. It has long been understood that, across the vast geography of modern America, the media constitutes the public square. With globalization, that is now truer for the world as a whole. Movies, music, the Internet, and popular culture, as Gore Vidal has put it, are "the new Agora."

Alongside our military, economic, scientific, and technological prowess, the reach and content of American mass culture itself has become a factor in international relations. Since the new politics of global culture is about whose story wins on the world stage, Hollywood is, for better and worse, a major player in that contest. The winners always write the script of history, as Hollywood did for decades. Now, with the democratization of the global media and the shift of power to many centers – the rise of the rest – history has many auteurs.

## Notes

1. Kermode, F. (2008) "Ezra Conquers London." *New York Review of Books*, vol. 55, no. 7.
2. Armitage, R. L., and Nye, J. S. (2007) *A Smarter, More Secure America*. CSIS Commission on Smart Power 17.
3. *Pew Research Center Publications*, November 7, 2007.

4.   Gardels, N. "Europe Needs A Little Obamainia." *Huffington Post,* July 14, 2008.

5.   Moïsi, D. "Obama Holds Up Mirror to the French." *Financial Times,* June 9, 2008.

6.   Oates, J. C. "The Human Idea." *The Atlantic,* November 2007.

7.   Scowcroft, B. (2007) "The Dispensable Nation?" *New Perspectives Quarterly,* vol. 24, no. 4, pp. 31–4.

8.   Ebadi, S. (2004) "America No Longer the Standard for Human Rights." *New Perspectives Quarterly,* vol. 21, no. 3, pp. 11–12.

9.   Smale, A. "U.S. Image Abroad Hard to Fix, Longtime Ally Says." *New York Times,* March 13, 2008.

10.  Blitz, J. "US Faces 'Long Struggle' to Overcome Worldwide Hostility." *Financial Times,* November 6, 2007.

11.  Gapper, J. "Sex and the City Guide to Media." *Financial Times,* May 14, 2008.

12.  Gatsiounis, I. "Hollywood Still Seduces the World: Global Anti-Americanism Aside, US Films Sell More Tickets Abroad Than at Home." *YaleGlobal,* February 7, 2008.

13.  Bayles, M. "The Ugly Americans: How Not to Lose the Global Culture War." *AEI Online,* December 4, 2006.

14.  Bayles, M. "The Ugly Americans: How Not to Lose the Global Culture War." *AEI Online,* December 4, 2006.

15.  "The Internet in China: Alternative Reality." *The Economist,* February 2, 2008, 65–6.

16.  Bayles, M. "Goodwill Hunting." *The Wilson Quarterly,* Summer 2005.

17.  Gerecht, R. M. "Mirror-Imaging the Mullahs: Our Islamic Interlocutors." *World Affairs,* Winter 2008.

18.  "Hollywood Disinformation." *New Perspectives Quarterly* (Fall 1998), vol. 15, no. 5.

19.  "There Are No Shortcuts to the End of History." Interview with Nathan Gardels. *New Perspectives Quarterly* (Spring 2006), vol. 23, no. 2, pp. 34–8.

20.  Andrews, H. "Muslim Women Don't See Themselves as Oppressed, Survey Finds." *New York Times,* June 8, 2006.

21.  Maria Shriver's Women's Conference (2007). Unpublished Speech. Long Beach.

22.  Bayles, M. "Risky Business for Hollywood." *International Herald Tribune,* May 8, 2008.

23. Ratzinger, J. and Pera, M. (2007) *Without Roots: The West, Relativism, Christianity, Islam.* Perseus.

24. Joffe, J. "The Perils of Soft Power." *New York Times Magazine*, May 14, 2006.

25. Gardels, N. (1995) "The East Asian Way." Interview with Nathan Gardels, in *At Century's End.* Alti.

26. Slackman, M. "Young Saudis, Vexed and Entranced by Love's Rules." *New York Times*, May 12, 2008.

27. Gardels, N. "China's Open Underground, Taiwan's Aperture." *New Perspectives Quarterly* (Winter 2008), vol. 25, no. 1, pp. 117–23.

28. Mahbubani, K. (2008) *The New Asian Hemisphere: The Irresistible Shift of Global Power to the East.* Public Affairs, p. 7.

# Chapter 3

# Creativity into Cash:
# How Hollywood Works

As familiar as the world is with Hollywood's products, far less is understood about the crucible in which these products are forged, the often messy nexus between creativity and commerce in which the cultural sausage is made.

This chapter examines the forces within that crucible which ultimately determine whether what comes out on the screen for the world to see is mangled drama, morally depraved *oeuvre*, or masterpiece. Why does Hollywood create what it does? What is the motivation? How is it done?

Everything that comes out of Hollywood comes in the name of entertainment. Everything serves the bottom line. The movie business is just that – a business. Creativity may be the motive on one side, but Hollywood is all about translating that creativity into cash. And, of course, even those in it for the art immensely enjoy the sense of freedom power, money, and fame bring. Within this nexus there are independent films, which are financed differently and may or may not get into a diminishing number of distribution companies. Many more films get made that never find theatrical distribution.

The decision to make or not make a film is highly speculative. If you have been around long enough, you learn that success is always a surprise because no one who decides what product gets made knows anymore than anyone else what will work in the future, what story will strike a nerve and haul in the audiences. Usually, marketing studies about the *last* success rather than the creative potential of the next project are decisive in studios making decisions on what to make. Today, most films have a short shelf-life, but when the quality is high enough, that life can extend on for years, if not decades.

In this process "zeitgeist" – catching the cultural moment – plays a big part in success. That includes the timing of a release and the belief in the film by its distributor, which is reflected in how well they execute their promotional campaign with the muscle and money they put behind the film. Zeitgeist also includes the currency of the subject matter at the time of its release, how truthful and real it feels to an audience, which can sense a fake long before it opens. Finally, success can depend on what films it is opening against. Deciding when to open a picture becomes a very important element that may determine its success.

Facing these constraints, several of the most highly acclaimed films in Hollywood history nearly never were. *Apocalypse Now*, for example, almost didn't get made, and for the usual reason. No one wanted to finance this now classic tale of how brutalizing war could turn a gung-ho patriot of the John Wayne stripe (who, incidentally never served in the armed forces) into the shadowy hulk of Marlon Brando demented by his own surprising capacity for evil in the darkest recesses of the jungle.

The film was only possible because Francis Ford Coppola had made *The Godfather* and *The Godfather II*, two classic films about the Italian mafia. It also helped that he provided a portion of the financing himself by pre-selling the rights in some foreign markets. After being turned down by Steve McQueen and Robert Redford, neither of whom wanted to spend what was thought to be four months in the jungle, he landed Marlon Brando as co-star in the film with a promise that he would only have to spend four weeks on the set. It turned out to be a two-year stint for all the other actors.

*Coming Home* was made partly because one of the authors had been Jane Fonda's agent and Hal Ashby, the director, Waldo Salt, the writer, and everyone involved was willing to make what was, for them, a labor of love. Not insignificantly, the film was priced right because Fonda was really committed to a process of not only healing the domestic wounds of war, but of also showing that the war continued on the home front for those who had been physically and mentally maimed in Vietnam.

Ernst Goldschmidt, the head of the International Division at Orion at the time, was interested in doing Oliver Stone's *Platoon* because it made economic sense for the company to get this film for a mere $2.5 million investment. No other company wanted the film because no one anticipated its success.

*Platoon* was financially the most successful of these three Vietnam war films, probably because it was made in 1986, long after the war. The other two movies were made while the wounds of that divisive and unpopular war were still raw. All reflected the shifting mood of the country, but all were done, from the producer's standpoint, for commercial reasons, not politics. The low costs protected the studio from the risk of total failure.

The point is that even behind these strongly politically oriented films, Hollywood is a hard-nosed business beholden to very real financial imperatives above and beyond the glitz, glamour, artistic impulse, or political leaning. At the beginning and end of the day Hollywood is about making money through entertainment – good entertainment if possible, bad or even embarrassing if profitable.

Of course, Hollywood has always been about making money. But since these three Vietnam films were made, the sausage factory of entertainment has changed even more dramatically. Once upon a time the old guard of Hollywood's elite studio heads had a personal investment in the economic success of their films and their companies. That Samuel Goldwyn put up his own house as collateral to get one of his films financed is a Hollywood legend. Like others in his day, his company was privately owned and he didn't answer to stockholders or to giant parent companies like Sony, as is the case today. The cost of production, distributing, and marketing the product today is extremely high. Companies are either already dependent on outside financing, or require outside funding as part of their business plan, to be competitive. Since the year 2000, according to UBS research $15 billion of outside capital has come into Hollywood.

"Few people today view running a studio as the ultimate career achievement," Patrick Goldstein has written. "Those glory days are long gone. Today's studio bosses are managers, not owners. They don't make movies. They preside over the creation of franchises, running a company that is a tiny sliver of some giant media conglomerate's overall business,"[1] albeit a very visible part of it. Notable exceptions include MGM and Lion's Gate, which are pure motion picture companies.

In short, studios today are run by hired guns who inhabit rented chairs, by marketing mavins focused on what succeeded in the past instead of what might work next, and video and foreign sales experts more familiar with spreadsheets than scripts. Studios today deal with such large sums of money that bankers and private investors are a part of the whole decision-making process. In most cases, these people want creative as well as fiscal control, though they have never actually made a film themselves.

Instead of taking creative risks, they conduct economic sensitivity studies in an attempt to plot a film's prospective success on a grid. They base decisions on hindsight because they can't project with certainty what will catch fire for a movie that takes a year to make from filming to release. It's safer to go for high-concept mega-hit movies which are salable because a movie's logline, often described as "content" by the bean counters, seems to be a safer bet despite its cost. This is the current trend.

Despite all this, those who produce what comes out of Hollywood today aspire to the head rented chair. After all, that chair has the best pay package and perks – private planes, boats, and automobiles, the best hotels, and beautiful homes with screening rooms. Yet it's difficult to run a business model in which you try to hit home runs too many times. The likelihood is that you will strike out more often than not. No one makes money trying to outguess the public even when creativity, passion, understanding of the future, and telling good and different stories seems to be the smartest route.

Oliver Stone may have leveled the most acid critique at his own industry, which he nonetheless relies upon to propagate his own truths. "All the crap that is produced, especially on television, is to keep the masses entertained every day and every week, like the Roman Circus. Bottom line, the problem with the American media today is that it is driven by money."[2]

As is his wont, Stone puts a dark and dramatic cast on things. You could say it another way: Hollywood produces as much art as commerce will allow; it allows as much politics and social commentary as entertainment can bear. Pure and simple, that is the mandate of the box office. Any story brought to the screen must pass through this unyielding filter before it comes out the other side into the public consciousness.

Despite the dictatorship of the bottom line, of course, "accidents do happen; good films can be made in Hollywood," as the Greek filmmaker Constantin Costa-Gavras once quipped.³ When that happens, as with the Vietnam films we discussed, what emerges can both powerfully reflect as well as shape the tenor of the times, for audiences at home as well as abroad. Movies are, in effect, a pictorial index of time.

"The business of films is the business of dreams," Nathaniel West once wrote. "We translate and interpret and transfer from films back to life, but we do it instantly and intuitively, working at a level of awareness somewhere just below full consciousness. Much of our experience of popular films – and of popular culture generally: jokes, plays, novels, songs, night-club acts, television shows and series – resides in the place we usually call the back of the mind, the place where we keep all those worries that won't come out into the open and won't go away either, that nag at us from the edges of consciousness."⁴

Big production films can consolidate a mood in America and reflect that mood abroad to others. In his 2008 book *Pictures At A Revolution* Mark Harris makes just this case – that key films in 1968 set the tone of the times, both reflecting and helping to unleash a broad anti-war and racial justice sentiment in America. *Bonnie and Clyde*, ostensibly about gangsters in new-wave cinema style, became a critique of violence and celebration of rebellion. *Guess Who's Coming to Dinner* and *In the Heat of the Night* became eloquent propaganda for civil rights, with many actors from the era like Sidney Poitier, Harry Belafonte, and Sammy Davis moving from the screen to the streets.

This same dynamic was evident in the 2006 awards season. The liberal membership of the Academy of Motion Picture Arts and Sciences, which grants the Oscars, rewarded the most charming and handsome among them, George Clooney, for daring to stand up to the then conservative mood of the country with his films *Good Night and Good Luck* and *Syriana*.

Clooney's acceptance speech for best supporting actor on Oscar night didn't disappoint them either. The suave celebrity, who played an earnest CIA operative whom big oil companies tried to cynically manipulate for their own ends, gave a rousing hurrah to his fellow stars and filmmakers. In a sardonic nod to conservative critics, he praised Hollywood for being so "out of touch" with America that it was able to alert the otherwise slumbering Republic to the perils ahead. No doubt he had in mind not only films such as *In the Heat of the Night* or *Guess Who's Coming to Dinner*, but also *To Kill A Mockingbird* which, with Gregory Peck in the lead role, helped install that warm voice of essential decency in the collective American conscience. There were also later films like *Philadelphia*, in which the familiar face of Tom Hanks brought awareness of the AIDS epidemic to audiences everywhere.

And now *Good Night and Good Luck* warned of the erosion of civil liberties in the face of fear. *Syriana* laid bare the raw interests that have kept America mired in Middle East turmoil for decades, most recently in Iraq.

Most of the films that come out of Hollywood, of course, are not so straightforwardly political or focused on social themes, but entertaining dramas or action films which more easily fit with the imperatives of the box office. Yet, it is such movies as *The Simpsons*, which uses often adolescent humor to explore the transformation of contemporary family life, or *Titanic*, which wraps the tensions of class and mobility in a tragic historical event, that have the biggest impact on audiences. Both transmit "second order" information about the assumptions Americans have about themselves and the world at large.

The fact that they fit the mold by turning creativity into lots of cash in many ways only magnifies their importance as building blocks of the American narrative.

## Notes

1. Goldstein, P. "Can She Restore the Roar?" *Los Angeles Times,* March 18, 2008.
2. Stone, O. "The Media Beast." *New Perspectives Quarterly* (Fall 1998), vol. 15, no. 5, p. 40.
3. Gardels, N. (ed.) (1997) "Resisting the Colonels of Disney." Interview with Nathan Gardels, in *The Changing Global Order.* Blackwell, p. 230.
4. Wood, M. (1975) *America in the Movies.* Basic Books, Inc., pp. 16–17.

# Chapter 4

# Seeing and Being Seen

## America Sees the World Through Movies

Over the past 100 years, Hollywood entertainment, whether through films with strong social and political themes or just pure entertainment, has played an immense role in cumulatively shaping the operative metaphors for Americans about the world beyond our experience just as they have shown America to the outside. In short, far more than the history books or journalistic media, Hollywood has been our means of seeing and being seen in the world.

This chapter is not an exhaustive film history nor a comprehensive survey of America's past efforts at public diplomacy. Rather it is an impressionistic account meant to illustrate the interconnections between the two.

Inevitably, as the French scholar Jean-Michael Valantin has argued, American movies have tended, recurrently, to reveal the culture's preoccupation with its "frontier" and "manifest destiny" myths, the battle between good and evil and "threats" from the outside whether the yellow peril of Fu Man Chu or, in later times, Saddam-looking thugs who reaffirm America's sense of identity as the exceptional guardian of the right way among nations. Valantin's frame is a good one and we follow it roughly throughout this chapter. Indeed, the opening voiceover of the *Superman* TV series that ran throughout the 1950s and early 60s proclaims Clark Kent's unique superpowers are employed in the service of "truth, justice, and the American way."

The myth of the lone cowboy making his own way out there on the limitless frontier of American possibility, creating a just order out of coarse human endeavor amid vast open ranges, is the mythic theme of countless Westerns from *Gunfight At The OK Corral* to *The Great Train Robbery* to *High Noon* to the TV series *Gunsmoke* or *Bonanza*, reportedly Osama bin Laden's childhood favorite. All deal with good versus evil, adventure and the law.

Clint Eastwood, of course, epitomizes this role. The myth is so powerful in the American psyche that Henry Kissinger famously cast himself to the Italian journalist Orianna Fallaci in the heroic, lone cowboy role even though the closest he ever came to an equine experience was studying Napoleon on horseback at Harvard.

As Woodrow Wilson extolled America's role in bringing democracy and self-determination to the world in the early twentieth century, Charlie Chaplin followed with a complementary, personalized face of America as a rising power in the world. Through the new medium of silent films he became the first global celebrity. His pro-little guy, anti-authoritarian politics, which jibed perfectly with Wilsonian ideals, were as familiar to his audiences, at home as well as globally, as his penguin shuffle, humorous facial ticks, mustache, cane, and top hat. If America was the maker of the modern world, Chaplin's later film, *Modern Times* (1936) was the story told on screen. Chaplin even tried to use his global celebrity to diminish Hitler through humor in *The Great Dictator*.

Later, in the immediate post-World War II period, Hollywood began to tell the stories shared collectively by so many war veterans who were now returning to their families and normalcy, codifying in images, in a way history books never could, the experience of sacrifice and triumph in the national psyche. John Wayne's *Sands of Iwo Jima* comes immediately to mind. *Sayanora*, with Red Buttons as an American soldier falling in love with a Japanese girl, signaled in popular culture the reconciliation with Japan that was taking place in diplomacy. Much later films, such as *Battle of the Bulge* (1965), *Where Eagles Dare* (1969), *Tora Tora Tora* (1970), and *Patton* (1976) more or less closed out the WWII chapter until Steven Spielberg's *Saving Private Ryan* in 1998 and Terrence Malick's *The Thin Red Line* (1998).

As the ground was laid by the Eisenhower era for a *Leave it to Beaver* life in the wake of the Korean conflict, Hollywood, like America as a whole, shifted its attention to the nuclear anxieties of the Cold War with the Soviets and Chinese.

The McCarthy hearings and the studio blacklists, which sought to root out Communist Party members in Hollywood, were perhaps the seminal recognition in Washington of the power of storytellers over the American narrative. It was one thing to have spies in the State Department where they had access to diplomatic secrets, but to allow talented moviemakers access to the impressionable minds of the public was a really serious matter. The wounds caused by these hearings haunted and split Hollywood for decades afterward. This was clearly evident the night Elia Kazan, the great director of *On The Waterfront*, was given an honorary award and members of the audience, who considered him unethical for naming names of suspected Communist Party members, sat with their arms folded.

Films like the *Manchurian Candidate* and *Dr. Strangelove* explored the paranoia and fears of those times when schoolchildren hid under desks in nuclear attack drills, which escalated during the Kennedy Administration with the Cuban missile crisis and the Khrushchev challenge to the Western presence in Berlin. *Dr. Strangelove* is essentially a story of Cold War politics that portrayed each side as loony as the other. *Invasion of the Body Snatchers* evoked the paranoia of the times; the pods were an allegory for communist automatons taking away personal freedom and sedating the masses. *On the Beach*, with Gregory Peck and Ava Gardner, took a post-holocaust look at nuclear war in 1959, as did many later films such as *Planet of the Apes* (1968), *The Day After* in 1983, and even *Terminator I* and *Terminator II* (1990s) which also told a post-holocaust story of war with surviving machines made in man's image.

It was during the tensest days of the Cold War that John Kennedy, enamored of Hollywood like his father, suggested to Arthur Krim, then Chairman of United Artists, that Ian Fleming's 007 espionage novels ought to be made into movies, bringing that James Bond glamour to the struggle against the Russians. It was also just in the wake of Kennedy's thousand days that John Wayne's patriotic Green Beret films hit theaters, casting counterinsurgency in the Asian jungles as a continuation of America's fight for freedom against fascism. Wayne obtained the cooperation of the Pentagon by writing to LBJ, arguing the importance of "telling the story of our troops." Wayne wanted to show the world why we were in Vietnam and set apart military wisdom from the incompetence of the President's civilian advisers. For him the best way to fight the liberal critics was with a movie.

As the anti-Vietnam war movement and the counterculture erupted in the Johnson and Nixon years, Hollywood loomed large with films like *Easy Rider* which iconified the youth rebellion and disaffection with the "new south" and the silent majority rising in resentment against the counterculture. The film was a dream for the studios – it struck a deep chord among audiences and only cost $1 million to make.

With a certain cultural lag, this was followed with a cinema of catharsis and healing, expressed in the films we have discussed like *Apocalypse Now* and *Coming Home*. Memorably, *Deer Hunter* and *Coming Home* battled it out not only for Oscar nominations – *Deer Hunter* won best film, and best director for Michael Cimino, while *Coming Home* won best actors for Jane Fonda and Jon Voight – but in public opinion. *Deer Hunter* had a hawkish cast that demonized the Vietnamese in a famous Russian roulette scene that actually never happened except in the movie; *Coming Home* was about how the foolish policies of the best and brightest wrecked the lives of promising young men who came home as broken veterans of a war everyone wanted to forget.

Stanley Kubrick's film *Full Metal Jacket* portrayed the same naïve arrogance George W. Bush would later hold with regard to Iraq that inside every Vietnamese there is an American trying to get out.

Though Vietnam was by that point the most televised war in history, with the effect of forcing President Johnson to step down from power, it was left to the storytellers in Hollywood to sort it out with their audiences about what it all meant in the end.

As Hollywood labored to put more recent political history and its consequences on the screen, the reaction in politics, fueled by distaste for the chaotic '60s and instigated by the humiliation of the Iranian hostage crisis, set in with the election of Ronald Reagan. This era of recovering American patriotic manhood and "standing tall" found its Hollywood emblem not just in an actor in the White House, but particularly in the Rambo movies. At a time when the US was waging the last fight of the Cold War in Nicaragua, one could find Rambo videos and posters in shops across the world from Cairo to Bangkok.

Indeed, Reagan's revived, post-detente anti-Sovietism found widespread expression in Hollywood with films like John Milius's *Red Dawn* (1984) and Chuck Norris in *Invasion USA* (1985), even *Rocky* (1985), in which Sylvester Stallone duked it out with a Russian boxer. In this refrosted era, apropos a Hollywood actor in the White House, politics took on some Hollywood labels. Reagan adviser Richard Perle earned the epithets "the prince of darkness" and "Darth Vader" (also Dick Cheney's screen name) from the *Star Wars* series. The central plank of Reagan's second term in office, the Strategic Defense Initiative, became known popularly as "star wars." Much later, in 2006, as the mood along the Potomac soured over the Iraq war, top CIA officials told the *Washington Post*'s Bob Woodward that "it was like *Mad Max* over there," referring to the film in which Mel Gibson's starred as a marauder in a post-apocalypse desert. As so often, film dialogue becomes part of the popular lexicon, shared mass metaphor.

Though the drama of the end of the fall of the Berlin Wall and the collapse of the Soviet Union was the most important historical event since World War II, it seemed, oddly, to find little expression in Hollywood, which had, in its Rambo mode, reduced the world to villains and good guys. Scriptwriters were at a seeming loss when the bad guys disappeared. The suave bravado of Sean Connery as James Bond became "boozy Blair," who, in *Russia House*, sold out not his country, but the hypocrisy of the military industrial complex that didn't want the Cold War to end, for a lovely Russian woman and a deeply disillusioned nuclear scientist who took glasnost more seriously than it was taken by the cynical Western intelligence agencies.

A series of Cold War echo films by Tom Clancy hit the screen even as Reagan himself strolled with Gorbachev in Red Square and the Soviet empire began to visibly come apart. These films included *The Hunt for Red October* (1990), *Crimson Tide* (1995), and *Patriot Games* (1992). A few small films, like Oliver Stone's *Salvador*, examined the last throes of Cold War guerilla conflict in the far corners of the world.

The dilution of the global confrontation of pure good and evil in the fuzzy Bush Sr. years when Gorbachev became our friend continued through Clinton when the only political themes Hollywood could find were White House farces such as Gary Ross's *Dave* with Kevin Kline and Sigourney Weaver. How could you dramatize an administration foreign policy concerned mainly with consolidating democracy in a now liberated Eastern Europe, trade, and jobs? How could you make a feature film for a PG13 audience that portrayed Monica giving Bill a blow job in the Oval Office? In *Wag the Dog*, foreign policy – a faux war – appeared only as a ruse to distract the public from domestic shenanigans bringing down the powers that be.

Two films of note dealt with Bush Sr.'s first Gulf War. *True Lies* with Arnold Schwarzenegger, included Mesopotamian bad guys; *Three Kings* (1999) told the weird tale of a war half fought under black billows of burning oil in a strange land. The latter is a wonderful example of what Hollywood can do when it puts its mind to it. Even the tiny details of graffiti and regional accents in Iraq were accurate.

The Balkan wars were perhaps too complex and brief, historically speaking, to warrant Hollywood's or the public's attention, save for *Behind Enemy Lines*, an episode about the military's resolve to get back one lost pilot. The James Bond series also turned, briefly, to the search for new threats in rogue Russian generals trying to keep the balance of terror alive past its time, later shifting to a spoiled red prince from North Korea. *The Bourne Supremacy* also touched on the theme of corrupted former Cold Warriors conspiring to make a few bucks at the expense of global security. Perhaps presciently, *Pearl Harbor* (2000) returned to the theme of surprise attack on an innocent, unsuspecting America distracted by the pursuit of happiness. "Threat cinema" otherwise moved on to otherworldly or natural disasters for a while with films such as *Independence Day* (1996) with alien attacks, and *Deep Impact* (1998) about a meteor hit that causes the sea to wash over Manhattan.

In some ways Hollywood, more than the CIA, intuited what Osama bin Laden had in mind for America. In *Debt of*

*Honor* (1995), a 747 crashes into the US Congress when the president is delivering his annual address. In the *Sum of All Fears* (2002), which hit screens just after 9/11 but was in production long before, Tom Clancy had to change the original Palestinian terrorists in his plot so as not to offend Arabs at such a delicate moment.

Only recently did the film industry get its groove back on this new conflict with Islamist terrorists. Like *Flight 93*, Oliver Stone's *World Trade Center*, sought to position 9/11 in the new American psyche as a trial met with courage by the common man facing a ruthless, unfathomable enemy. As reinforced by the experience of films such as *Rendition*, *Redacted*, *Lions for Lambs*, *The Valley of Elah* (2007), or *Stop-Loss* (2008), the mediocre box office take suggests that not all that many Americans want to review bad headlines in the cinema without more emotional distance.

In 2005–8 one important development worth noting was the emergence of documentaries by Hollywood figures addressing key issues from the war in Iraq, such as Michael Moore's *Farenheit 9/11*, to Leo DiCaprio's *The 11ᵗʰ Hour* on climate change and, of course, Al Gore's *An Inconvenient Truth*, produced by Lawrence Bender, who also produced Quentin Tarantino's films *Kill Bill Vol. 1 & 2* and *Pulp Fiction*. Certainly, as such films grow in polished technique and audience share they will be a continuing part of Hollywood's influential output.

As we will discuss in a subsequent chapter, aside and beyond the 9/11 experience, globalization has now roared through Hollywood like every other industry, upsetting old patterns of distribution and production with the digital democratization of the media – "everyone is their own film-maker now" – and bringing new global tales like *Babel*, instead of American-centered narratives, to the big screen. With the growing importance of foreign markets, iconic

American companies like Disney, Fox, and Sony are even trying to re-brand themselves as "global" through local production partnerships in India and China.

Inexorably, by transforming the tales Hollywood tells, globalization will transform the way Americans see themselves as part of the world instead of, as this selective film review has suggested, being apart from it.

## Movies and Public Diplomacy: The World Looks At America

How the rest of the world sees America in the future will also change as the consequences of globalization seep into the media diets of audiences everywhere. But their point of departure is what they have already seen coming out of Hollywood over the last few decades – including through official efforts at public diplomacy that have sought to leverage the power of the manufactured image in America's foreign policy interests while helping expand markets for American movies.

Hollywood had long made its mark from the advent of silent films, but the cultural confidence that came with triumph against Germany and Japan under-girded America's new-found economic and political prowess, which in turn enabled Hollywood's growing success.

In the wake of that devastating war, America came out on top. It was the great power with the happy ending. American films in English with subtitles or dubbed became the standard in many countries. English became the lingua franca. This real-world dominance in turn translated into the capacity to expand distribution outlets globally as the US government used the clout of the Marshall Plan's largesse as well as market-opening mandates for screening American films in the prostrate economies of Europe and Asia.

A star system with worldwide appeal was established thanks to the optimistic savvy of a marketing system that sold the message of glamour and success on the silver screen to a down-and-out global public that yearned for it.

Writing about America's rising image in the post-WWII era Martha Bayles has argued that "it is hard to see how the contest for popular opinion [in the world] could have been won in those years without such vibrant and alluring cinematic products as *Singin in the Rain* (1952), *On the Waterfront* (1954), *Twelve Angry Men* (1967), *Some Like It Hot* (1959), or *The Apartment* (1960)."[1]

Understanding this, Washington eagerly sought to employ Hollywood's influence to win hearts and minds abroad as well as bolster public opinion at home in favor of foreign policy objectives. These efforts intensified as the Cold War took hold, but had their roots going back to the birth of Hollywood and the first American "propaganda minister" under Woodrow Wilson. At key moments, the US government helped win global markets for American entertainment in return for the propaganda value films and music provided.

In 1917, Woodrow Wilson established the Committee on Public Information to enlist a fledgling Hollywood's talents in making films such as *The Hun* and *The Kaiser: The Beast of Berlin*, that supported the cause of joining the war. The CPI chairman, George Creel, also baldly believed that Hollywood movies could "carry the gospel of Americanism to every corner of the globe."[2] Although the CPI was shut down after World War I, Washington rewarded Hollywood by forcing open markets in a Europe devastated by war – one reason why, by the 1920s, American films were already making 35 percent of revenues abroad. By 1925, American films captured 70 percent of the market in France.[3]

World War II revived the link between Washington's war efforts and Hollywood's persuasive capacities with anti-fascist films that ranged from *Why We Fight* by Frank Capra to the Warner brother's films *Confessions of a Nazi Spy* and *Mission to Moscow.* Though initially Washington was mainly concerned with mobilizing Americans for war, the State Department quickly came to see the value of American movies in helping win over hearts and minds in contested zones as the war wound down. Roosevelt's Office of War Information, in fact, sent movies and Coca-Cola to woo liberated populations in France and Italy into the American camp.

As after WWI, Hollywood's reward came again in the form of greater access to new markets in a world where local cultures had been broken by war. As Richard Pells recounts in his book *Not Like Us*, one of the first pieces of legislation aimed at helping Hollywood secure a European presence after the war was the Informational Media Guarantee Program of 1948 in which the US government guaranteed the reimbursement of Hollywood studios in dollars for their earnings in non-convertible European currencies.

The quid pro quo for this deal, according to Pells, was that the State Department wanted Hollywood to export films that "reflected favorably" on the US, with "less gangsters, less violence and positive depictions of Americans." In particular they didn't want any films that might feed the Communist critique of America's raw capitalism such as *The Grapes of Wrath*, which the Motion Picture Association agreed to withdraw from export. Nonetheless, Pells notes, films in many ways just as unflattering to American life, at least for those innocent times, got through. These included *Double Indemnity, Sunset Blvd., All About Eve, High Noon, On the Waterfront, Rebel Without A Cause, East of Eden, Psycho,* and *Splendor in the Grass,* among others.

A State Department memo in 1948 expressed Washington's newfound enthusiasm for employing Hollywood's influence on audiences abroad instead of at home: "American motion pictures, as ambassadors of good will, interpret the American way of life to all the nations of the world, which may be invaluable from a political, cultural and commercial point of view."[4] With markets broadly opened to American films and mass culture generally, public diplomacy's alliance with American mass culture kicked into high gear in 1953 when the United States Information Agency was established as the Cold War was heating up. The intelligence community also got involved.

According to Hugh Wilford's history of the CIA's efforts to covertly influence public opinion, *The Mighty Wurlitzer,*[5] project Militant Liberty was established in 1954 as a multi-agency propaganda effort to use movies as a means to "embed American-style democratic values in foreign cultures, especially in new theaters of the Cold War as Central America, the Middle East and Southeast Asia." An informal group known as "the Hollywood consortium" advised the project. Among those included in the group were the director John Ford, the actor John Wayne, Cecil B. DeMille and Twentieth Century Fox studio chief Daryl Zanuck. "We need to make certain our films are doing a good job for our nation and our industry," foreign marketing specialist Eric Johnston said of the group's objective.[6]

During this same period the Psychological Warfare Workshop of the CIA not only tried to insert "the right ideas" into Hollywood scripts, according to Wilford, but also initiated projects, including an animated version of *Animal Farm* written by George Orwell, under a shell company called Touchstone. Among the more notorious interventions was a suggestion that the ending of Orwell's story be amended so that the pigs and dogs would face a liberation-style uprising of the other animals – a strategy that allegorized the intelligence agencies' strategy at the time to roll back Communist power in Eastern Europe.

Wilford also contends that the CIA actually had an agent at Paramount Studios in Hollywood to try to keep scripts on track with American foreign policy objectives, for example advising that "the manhandling of Moslem women" in a Jerry Lewis and Dean Martin comedy *Money From Home*, might cause a negative reaction in the Muslim world. The agent also noted that a movie planned by Billy Wilder about the illegitimate Japanese child of an American GI would be "a wonderful piece of propaganda for the Communists."[7]

According to the original investigation by David Eldridge, which Wilford cites, the CIA agent at Paramount turned out to be Luigi G. Luraschi, a Paramount executive and head of foreign and domestic censorship at the studio whose job description was "to iron out any political, moral or religious problems and get rid of the taboos that might keep the picture out of, say, France or India."[8] Other studios, apparently, had similar self-censoring executives as well. When the Motion Picture Association of America formed an International Committee in the later 1950s, it was chaired by Luraschi.

By 1955, cultural diplomacy extended beyond movies to include music. Notably, the Voice of America, a division of the USIA, promoted jazz – "the music of freedom" – to its 100 million listeners worldwide, 30 million in the Soviet bloc. If the Russian novelist Vassily Aksyonov is any guide, these broadcasts had their intended impact. They were "America's secret weapon number one," Aksyonov later said, "casting a kind of golden glow over the horizon."[9]

Whatever the promise of the Hollywood–Washington liaison in selling America to the world, it was mostly broken apart by Joseph McCarthy's search for communists among the screenwriters and filmmakers who he suspected of using their powers of celluloid persuasion to subvert national security.

In the 1960s John Kennedy tried to reinvigorate public diplomacy when famed journalist Edward R. Murrow was asked to head the USIA, by then a complex agency that included the Voice of America, a Motion Picture division, and a press operation that had personnel in 125 countries. Morrow was assisted by George Stevens Jr., a writer and producer who later founded the American Film Institute. Their admirable efforts in those years were fairly undone among many of the target audiences by 1967 when the secret CIA funding of the Congress for Cultural Freedom, which dated from before Kennedy's time and existed throughout his presidency, became known. The idea of the Congress had been to gather a constellation of high-profile writers and artists to build a consensus for the values of the liberal West against Soviet-style communism. The fact that it was secretly funded by a direct arm of American foreign policy completely undermined its credibility.

Just as official cultural diplomacy foundered, the spread of American pop culture exploded, not the least bit aided by government assistance, along with the worldwide youth rebellion. Though in one instance the USIA awkwardly considered lining up Joan Baez, the Beach Boys, and Santana to attend a rock concert in Leningrad under their sponsorship, it didn't come to pass. Of course, the lack of official sponsorship of rock n' roll did nothing to diminish the influence of the likes of Frank Zappa on East bloc rebels such as Vaclav Havel.

Only as Soviet power was on its last legs did Ronald Reagan, who believed through experience in the power of images and information, rearm the USIA by appointing his friend Charles Wick and bloating the budget to an all-time high of $882 million. There was some notable successes, including the production of *Let Poland Be Poland*, a TV show that included Frank Sinatra and Charlton Heston. By supporting Polish independence, it offered aid and comfort to Solidarity. Because of Wick's ideological narrowness, that too came to naught. Fearing that even the mild-mannered Walter

Cronkite would give aid and comfort to the Soviet enemy by opposing a US military buildup, Wick nixed a speaking tour under USIA sponsorship for the venerated broadcaster.

With the end of the Cold War, the Clinton administration folded the USIA into the State Department since the battle of ideas was considered wrapped up with the triumph of the West. Between 1993 and 2001, according to the Council on Foreign Relations, the budget for education exchanges, libraries, writers' tours, and translations was cut by one-third, from $349 million to $232 million.[10] Concerned mostly about trade, the Clinton administration focused on protection of "intellectual property" and opening new markets to Hollywood products, bolstered by the energetic efforts of Jack Valenti, the head of the Motion Picture Association of America, who knew the ways of Washington going back to his time there as a top adviser to President Lyndon Johnson.

That assumption that the battle of ideas had been won rapidly unraveled in the wake of 9/11, when President George Bush rejoined the battle for hearts and minds against radical Islam by first assigning advertising executive Charlotte Beers and later his long-time confidante Karen Hughes as head of the Office of Public Diplomacy and Public Affairs within the State Department.

Trying to blunt the source of Islamist animosity, the effort at first was aimed at explaining America to the Muslim world in the belief that if only they understood us they wouldn't hate us. Karl Rove even came out to Hollywood to enlist the help of the studios and TV producers. Wary of aligning too closely with George Bush and finding themselves as ignorant as Washington about how to communicate to the Muslim world, Hollywood mostly balked and then passed altogether on the idea as the slide toward war in Iraq changed the agenda.

A few, however, made the effort. Norm Pattiz, chairman of the powerful Westwood One radio network and a former

member of the US Broadcasting Board of Governors, an independent agency that replaced the broadcast arm of the USIA,
helped start Radio Sawa in 2001 as a way of promoting
American goodwill in the Arab world through the spread of
popular American music.

Pattiz also helped create a US-funded Arab satellite TV sta-
tion called Al Houra, broadcast entirely in Arabic, covering
22 countries in the Middle East and ultimately reaching 30
million viewers out of a population of 350 million. Research
showed that 70 percent of the audience found the news to be
reliable and credible though, of course, they were disposed in
the first place to support the United States compared with the
viewers of indigenous media such as Al Jazeera or Al Arabiya.

Al Houra's mission was to offer an example of the free
media in the American tradition. In the end, however, it too
was considered a failure because no amount of goodwill
broadcasting changed anyone's mind as long as what most
Arabs regarded as the occupation of Iraq and (in their view)
the unbalanced support of Israel continued as the core of
American policy. Most Arabs considered it propaganda.

When all is said and done, public or cultural diplomacy
which sought to influence the foreign public had its greatest
(although small) success through Voice of America during the
Cold War, mostly in zones where Hollywood films and
American mass culture generally were off limits due to censorship and lack of access to markets. But as the world loos-
ened up in the 1960s and as various information and cultural
revolutions swept the world, American movies and music
spread into ubiquity, terminally eclipsing the official institutions of public diplomacy.

For now, in the eyes of official Washington, "culture" has
once again, as in the Clinton years, become a mere commod-
ity to be promoted in the mix of American products sold
abroad in the ever-expanding quest for new markets. As Dan

Glickman, the head of the Motion Picture Association, said in 2008, some countries trying to block the export of American films – "the free flow of information" – in the name of cultural diversity reminded him of his time as agricultural secretary under Bill Clinton when "genetically modified foods" were opposed on the basis that they were culturally foreign. "It was déjà vu," he said.

For better and for worse, America's story, as we've only so briefly sketched in this chapter, is thus known to the world out there as much by what Hollywood projects as by what the State Department's public diplomats seek to portray.

Camille Paglia once said that, in the long perspective of cultural history stretching back to the Greeks, Hollywood will be remembered as the most important thing America gave the world in the twentieth century. The question is, what exactly has it given?

## Notes

1. Bayles, M. "Goodwill Hunting." *The Wilson Quarterly*, Summer 2005.
2. Bayles, M. "The Ugly Americans: How Not to Lose the Global Culture War." *AEI Online*, December 4, 2006.
3. Bayles, M. "The Ugly Americans: How Not to Lose the Global Culture War." *AEI Online*, December 4, 2006.
4. Bayles, M. "Goodwill Hunting." *The Wilson Quarterly*, Summer 2005.
5. Wilford, H. (2008) *The Mighty Wurlitzer: How the CIA Played America*. Harvard University Press, pp. 116–17.
6. Wilford, H. *The Mighty Wurlitzer*, pp. 117–18.
7. Wilford, H. *The Mighty Wurlitzer*, p. 120.
8. Eldridge, D. (2000) "Dear Owen: The CIA, Luigi Luraschi and Hollywood, 1953." *Historical Journal of Film, Radio and Television*, vol. 20, no. 2.
9. Bayles, M. "Goodwill Hunting." *The Wilson Quarterly*, Summer 2005.
10. Bayles, M. "The Ugly Americans: How Not to Lose the Global Culture War." *AEI Online*, December 4, 2006.

# chapter 5

# Hollywood Beats the Red Army: The Height of America's Cultural Appeal

On a spring day in 1986, a group of CIA analysts filed with some urgency into a conference room at the agency's secure Langley headquarters. They had been called together by one of the more far-sighted officials of the National Intelligence Council to discuss fresh, open source intelligence that undermined key assumptions about the Soviet Union. It was the first term of the Reagan administration and those manning the top ranks of the Pentagon and intelligence agencies were true believers who felt the era of detente had given the Evil Empire the upper hand. Only a new military buildup would hold the Soviets at bay.

In this light, the presentation was startling. Régis Debray, one of the world's most well-known radicals, an insider of the global revolution, old pal of Fidel, Che, and Salvador Allende as well as a top adviser to the socialist president of France, François Mitterrand, had said publicly what he had long believed privately: "There is more power in rock music videos, movies, blue jeans, fast food, news networks and TV satellites than in the entire Red Army."[1]

"Could Debray be right?" the analysts asked each other. "Are we missing something?"

They were indeed missing something. Debray was right. Within five years, the Soviet Union collapsed. In the event, one Russian wag endorsed Debray's point of view. "Rock n' roll," he said, "was the cultural dynamite that blew up the Iron Curtain."[2]

Of course, internal Soviet politics, including Gorbachev's policies of perestroika and glasnost, years of containment by NATO, the nuclear balance of terror with the US, and the draining effect of the war in Afghanistan counted greatly. But the legitimacy of the Soviet system was largely eroded over the decades by the incessant exposure to the freedoms of the West, including through the drumbeat of American mass culture and defection of its own cultural elites. Every time a Mikhail Baryshnikov, a Rudolf Nureyev or a Vladislav Rostropovich left for the West it was a blow against the system. Soft power had played a key role in defeating hard power.

The moment Debray described five years before the end of the Cold War probably marks the zenith of America's mass cultural influence globally.

The dreams of America – individual freedom, middle class prosperity, social mobility, the rule of law – were, to a great extent at that time, the dreams of the world. Even within the Soviet bloc, America, through its pop culture, was the proverbial beacon to audiences everywhere. Nixon may have lost the first TV clash with JFK, but he certainly bested Khrushchev in the fabled kitchen debate with the Soviet leader about standards of living. Pepsi Cola, Marlboro cigarettes, Elvis, jazz and later rock, the Rat Pack, the Ford Thunderbird, and *Gone with the Wind* blew away the competition.

Evidence of Hollywood's growing sway over hearts and minds in the 1950s and 1960s was easy to find.

As Marshall McLuhan recounted in his classic book, *Understanding Media*, one sweltering summer afternoon in 1956 a group of Hollywood executives made their way through the narrow, jammed streets of Jakarta's ramshackle shanties. They were headed to the presidential palace where Sukarno had invited them for a discussion about the future of Asia. Vietnam was heating up and the Malay Peninsula was in the full swing of an insurgency against the British.

When the studio chiefs arrived and were seated in a semicircle of overstuffed chairs, the hero of Third World nonalignment launched in with characteristic directness: "I regard you as political radicals and revolutionaries who have greatly hastened political change in the East," Sukarno seemed almost to scold them. "What the Orient sees in a Hollywood movie is a world in which all the ordinary people have cars and electric stoves and refrigerators. So the Oriental regards himself as an ordinary person who has been deprived of the ordinary man's birthright."

Sukarno clearly understood the mood of the people. Across the straits in Singapore, a young Kishore Mahbubani saw what Sukarno described. "I have vivid childhood memories," Mahbubani writes in his latest book, *The New Asian Hemisphere*, "of watching shows like *I Love Lucy* and *My Three Sons* on TV. They had a profound impact on me. I didn't really watch them for their stories. Instead I watched in amazement as the TV scenes showed row after row of suburban homes, each with a lawn and a driveway. All homes were equipped with refrigerators, TVs, telephones and washing machines (which I had never heard of). Miraculously, each home had one or two cars. Those scenes, which stood in sharp contrast to my own living circumstances – we had just gotten a flush toilet – provided me with a vision of what an ideal world could be."[3]

A world away, a young Constantin Costa-Gavras, who would later go on to make such classic movies as *Z*, which chronicles the overthrow of the democratic government in Greece, was similarly impressed as he drank in scenes from far away

Hollywood at his local Athens cinema: "The most political films I ever saw were those of Esther Williams, which I loved as a little boy. She was beautiful. She had the biggest car and the thickest carpets I had ever seen. Everybody looked wonderful. This was America!"[4] In this same way, American movies have captured the imagination of successive generations.

Decades after the Sukarno encounter, the spell of Hollywood was still working its magic on the hearts and minds of a global audience. In his brilliant travelogue of the late 1980s, *Video Night in Kathmandu*, Pico Iyer describes a scene in which villagers paid several rupees to gather around one of the handful of VCR's in the kingdom to watch a bad Indian imitation of Michael Jackson's contorted moves in "Thriller," entering the remote glamour of a world not their own. He also describes how a million Chinese raced to see Rambo in *First Blood* within ten days of its release, some paying seven times the official ticket price to hawkers.

In 1998, the journalist Orville Schell found the same phenomenon in the "faux location Himalayas" when he followed Brad Pitt around the Argentine Andes where *Seven Years in Tibet* was being filmed.

"Normally, Mendoza is a placid, provincial outpost centering around mining and vineyards," Schell reported. "But today the whole town is aflutter over 'Bread Peet.' His movie Seven has been showing here, and when 'Bread' himself arrived in the country it was as if the Dalai Lama had unexpectedly reappeared on Tibetan soil. He was chased across the airport tarmac by a group of teenage girls." "The whole place ees going crazee!" a leggy young woman waiting on tables in a downtown cafe told Schell.

"Even here in provincial Argentina," Schell summarized his encounter, "one feels the brute power of the American entertainment industry as it radiates out across the world from Hollywood's ground zero like shock waves from a blast site. From Lhasa to Lagos and Minsk to Mendoza, Brad Pitt is infinitely more fascinating and visible to ordinary people than any head of state, his global reach arguably as wide as that of the United States government and military combined."[5]

"Going crazee!" like the Argentine teenagers is also how one might describe the august European industrialists in Davos stumbling over each other to get a picture with Sharon Stone or Angelina Jolie whenever they grace the global business elite with their presence.

Even royalty is not immune. When King Hussein and Queen Noor visited Los Angeles in 1994, the royals' host, Stanley Sheinbaum, invited the Hollywood A list. Harrison Ford was there, and Barbra Streisand, as well as Arnold Schwarzenegger, among many others. They had come to see a real king who flew helicopters and fought wars. But it was King Hussein's many children who were all aflutter and star struck. They were meeting the modern royalty – Hollywood stars! The current king of Jordan, Abdullah, is an unabashed Trekkie who even appeared on one episode of *Star Trek Voyager*."[6]

As late as April 2006, "Brangelina" gave new hope to a downtrodden African continent suffering a fate worse than imperialism. As the *Washington Post* reported, quoting a breathless ambassador, Namibian officials hoped the world media furor over a visit by pregnant Hollywood star Angelina Jolie and her partner Brad Pitt would translate into a tourist rush to the African country, otherwise famous chiefly for its huge sand dunes and vast empty spaces.[7]

The Australian adventurer Paul Rafaelle recalled his return visit in the early 1990s to Timbuktu, the very emblem of remote geographic isolation, after many years. Yes, he still saw the nomads herding donkeys to the market as they had for centuries. But he also saw crowds of teenagers wearing LA Lakers shirts and mimicking the rap they'd seen on MTV since the arrival of cable! Timbuktu!

The list goes on in some surprising ways. Nasser's favorite movie was Frank Capra's *It's A Wonderful Life*, where an angel helps a compassionate but despairingly frustrated businessman by showing what life would had been like if he never existed.[8] The word around Hollywood was that North Korea's Kim Jong Il actually tried to get a role in a James Bond movie. Qiang Jing, or Madame Mao, regularly watched American movies at her private villas even as the Cultural Revolution against Western contamination raged across China. Fidel enthused to Francis Ford Coppola over *The Godfather*. And, according to Lawrence Wright in *The Looming Tower*, Osama bin Laden's favorite TV show as a kid growing up in Saudi Arabia was *Bonanza*, the same show we watched every Sunday night about a father and his sons doing the honorable thing with rugged independence when confronted by life's dilemmas out there on their frontier estate.

Surely, some of Hollywood's vast appeal is pure celebrity mania and being star struck, as may be the case with the Davos elites or with the Argentine teenagers. But much of it is undeniably the appeal of the American way of life that comes through, often incidentally, in all our films and pop music. Doubtless it is both to many.

Indeed, Michael Eisner of Disney was not off base when he said in 1995, that "the Berlin Wall was destroyed not by force of arms, but by the force of Western ideas. And what was the delivery system of those ideas? It has to be admitted that to an important degree it was American entertainment. Inherent in the best and worst of our movies and TV shows, books and records is a sense of individual freedom and the kind of life liberty can bring. It's in the films of Steven Spielberg; its in the humor of Bill Cosby. Its in the music of Madonna."[9]

Whatever the negative cultural consequences of the 1960s that would manifest themselves decades later, the eruption of freedom amid affluence from Berkeley to Paris, as well as the sex, drugs, and rock n' roll culture, appealed greatly to constrained youth everywhere in those years when America's global media presence exploded. For that moment, the ingestion of American pop culture globally seemed less a worry than the lethal spasms of closed societies in their last throes. Could there be any doubt that the Grateful Dead were preferable to the stiff ravens of the Politburo? As long as Brezhnev could still furrow his menacing eyebrows and send tanks into Prague, any and all the fruits of freedom were excused from judgment. This dynamic, no doubt, reinforced the infatuated embrace of American pop culture in its triumphant moment at the end of the Cold War, as Debray described.

Certainly, there is an essential message that comes across in America's cultural products, as Eisner rightly suggested.

One of the most compelling insights on this score was offered by the director Sydney Pollack whose many films included, *They Shoot Horses Don't They*, *Tootsie*, *Out of Africa*, and *The Interpreter*. Pollack died in 2008.

"The first filmmakers in America were immigrants," the seasoned director noted.

They were all looking for a way to speak to everybody, to find a lingua franca of stories and images that all Americans could relate to despite their linguistic and cultural backgrounds.

So, the first films were always basic kinds of morality plays, fables really, that pitted good against evil. There was always a hero and a damsel in distress. From those beginnings the vast movie industry was born, flourishing first in America and now everywhere in the world.

The world has gotten so small today we need some kind of similar lingua franca to communicate without having to penetrate the complicated depths of culture that insulate us from each other. American popular culture has done that now across the world.[10]

For Pollack there is little mystery to the appeal of American cinema.

> The prototypical hero in American films is going up against the odds and challenging authority. He or she is irreverent. These are surely admirable traits to young people who feel stifled by traditional culture. ... but there is another message as well: everything is possible. That is dramatic. American films say to people everywhere, "You don't have to be high and mighty to have a dramatic life." You may be a grade-school kid with braces on your teeth in some small town who dreams of getting out and having an adventure, making it in life. The movies tell you it is possible. You can write your own narrative. In a very fundamental way, this is what America itself is really all about.

This message of "writing your own narrative" is a message that permeates pop music as well. The fact that hip hop – the music of the marginalized underclass in the US – has become so popular in Africa or the Parisian suburbs is not surprising. But the fact that it is also the rage among Shanghai youth does suggest the broad and deep appeal of a culture in which the marginal can tell their own story, be heard and recognized.

As powerfully appealing as the message of personal liberty may be, the pervasive presence of the American medium that spreads it can as often as not seem suffocating to the makers of indigenous culture everywhere else, friend as well as foe.

## Notes

1.    "The Third World: From Kalashnikovs to God and Computers." Interview with Nathan Gardels. *New Perspectives Quarterly* (Spring 1986), vol. 3, no. 1, pp. 25–8.

2. Bayles, M. "Goodwill Hunting." *The Wilson Quarterly*, Summer 2005.
3. Mahbubani, K. (2008) *The New Asian Hemisphere: The Irresistible Shift of Global Power to the East*. PublicAffairs.
4. Gardels, N. (ed.) (1997) "Resisting the Colonels of Disney." Interview with Nathan Gardels, in *The Changing Global Order*. Blackwell, p. 231.
5. "The Third World: From Kalashnikovs to God and Computers." Interview with Nathan Gardels. *New Perspectives Quarterly* (Spring 1986), vol. 3, no. 1, pp. 25–8.
6. http://memory-alpha.org/en/wiki/Abdullah_ibn_al-Hussein.
7. Hannon, E. "Brangelina: Namibia's Biggest Game." *Washington Post*, May 28, 2006.
8. Zakaria, F. (2008) *The Post-American World*. W. W. Norton.
9. Gardels, N. (ed.) (1997) "Planetized Entertainment." Interview with Nathan Gardels, in *The Changing Global Order*. Blackwell, p. 228.
10. Peres, S. and Pollack, S. "Out of Hollywood." *New Perspectives Quarterly* (Fall 1998), vol. 15, no. 5.

# Chapter 6

## Backlash: Soft Power is Still Power, and Still Makes Enemies

When the winner takes all, including claims over the hearts and minds of a diverse world, it invites a backlash. Clearly, the dominant influence of American mass culture in the wake of the Cold War's end, quite apart from the ideas of democracy and individual freedom inherent in Hollywood films, TV shows, or even the art market, has caused a backlash precisely because of the diversity of identities unleashed by the defrosting of the bi-polar order.

Hence the sentiment expressed by Josef Joffe in Chapter 2 – that the growth of America's mass cultural presence into ubiquity in the era between the Vietnam and Iraq wars has generated resentment among those who sense an odor of occupation.

If there is resistance to military occupation, similarly there is resentment against cultural occupation. As much as global audiences have sucked up *Titanic* or global consumers have downloaded the latest Microsoft product, they want the cultural space to make their own choices. It is simply too overbearing for America to dominate the metaworld of information, icons, and entertainment as well as possess the world's top universities and technologies and, on top of that, spend more on our military than the next eight nations combined.

In a typical example of post-Cold War resentment, in June 2006, the Indonesian defense minister Juwono Sudarsono protested America's pervasive soft power. "The United States is overbearing and overpresent and overwhelming in every sector of life in many nations and cultures," he protested to America's then-secretary of hard power, Donald Rumsfeld.[1]

From Singapore to Ottawa, from Mexico City to Seoul, local cultural ministers, artists, filmmakers, and politicians have worried about their own cultural heritage being obliterated by the homogenizing, megastar, special-effects blockbusters that former Disney chief Michael Eisner once described as "planetized entertainment."

Acknowledging this issue, filmmaker Sydney Pollack agreed that America's mass cultural dominance must be "alarming" because "the power of the American industry pushes out the local films and flattens indigenous cultures … in so many countries the huge majority of film revenues are from American movies. In places like Greece and Germany, up to 80 per cent of films in theaters are American. People are abandoning their local cultures at the box office."[2]

For those critical of the American role in flattening global culture, Pollack honestly responded by cutting to the central conundrum of democratic culture which Hollywood, by and large, seems to have given up trying to figure out. "What kind of culture can you have in a society that celebrates the common man but doesn't like his tastes?" he asked. He continues:

In a democracy, at the end of the day, everybody's opinion is equal. Is it really possible to say, 'This is a society in which we won't tell you what to see, or what to do, you, the hero, the proletarian, the middle-class, the common man, but boy are you dumb and tasteless? Left to your own devices you will pick up the pulp novel and the worst movie

A film maker must live with that constraint. And, in a certain way, it does shape what Hollywood does. As an industry, it tends to pick for its projects what appeals most and offends least. The least challenging and the least provocative movie is the safest bet.

What then, is today's Hollywood? "What we are seeing now from Hollywood," Pollack offered with a certain sense of resignation,

is an "adolescizing of the world." The entertainment values that drive the industry are those of an adolescent: sex appeal and action. We are turning everybody into adolescents with MTV-style movies.

There are sherpas living in yurts who know as much about Tom Cruise as about their own culture. The spread of popular culture is a phenomenon that, while a big boon to the American economy, is a threat to a lot of other cultures – and to the maturity of our own.

In these comments, Pollack foreshadows the paradoxical issues that have emerged as American culture became ubiquitous. It may well spread a message of the promise of liberty, but douses by sheer scale other alternatives to entertainment increasingly geared to teen sensibilities.

Examples of resistance abound. South Korean filmmakers have not been alone in banding together to oppose a free-trade agreement with the United States which they feel would amount to "imperialism" over their industry.

When Alan Parker cast Madonna as Eva Peron in his film, *Evita*, Argentines all around were crying that their myths were being appropriated by Hollywood. The Peronist president at the time, Saul Menem, publicly announced his opposition to this act as "North American imperialism."

Jack Lang, who was France's Minister of Culture when Francois Mitterrand was president, remains the point man for European cultural resistance to America. His views are a kind of anti-Hollywood manifesto from the time when France still had a significant film industry, but nonetheless reflects the fervent notion that no one likes to be dominated. "Behind the glorious word 'universality' there are always forms of domination," he told the World Cultural Forum's first gathering in Venice in 1991. He continued:

> The Soviet empire that proclaimed – and enforced – a false universality has only just crumbled.
>
> Yet, shouldn't men and women of culture also fear that in the name of a new universality, vast financial groups and entertainment industries will impose cultural universality on a global scale?
>
> For the idea of "universality" not to betray us, it must be reached through the recognition of the identity of each and every one of us, not by criminal displacement of linguistic treasures and other diverse cultural forms.[3]

Lang was, of course, talking about Hollywood films which, even then, dominated the marquees at the movie cinemas along the Left Bank redoubt of St. Germain des Pres down the street from the Sorbonne.

Anticipating the satellite and digital age, Lang's eye was already on the future back in 1991. "And what about technology?" he asked doubtfully.

> Will technology enrich us by creating diversity of channels for more artistic expression, or might the truth be more ominous: the higher the satellite, the lower the culture?
>
> The disappearance of languages and cultural forms is the great risk today. Diversity threatens to be replaced by international mass culture without roots, soul, color or taste.

Despite Lang's eloquence, the tide for the moment seems to be flowing with those of his compatriots who have long mysteriously loved Jerry Lewis. America's perennial cultural critic is no doubt deeply dismayed these days by the French president, Nicolas Sarkozy, a fan of globalization who embodies the other side of the story. "We love the United States!" Sarkozy has enthused. "The dream of French families is to have their young people go to American universities to study. When we go to the movies, it is to see American films. When we turn on our radios, it is to listen to American music."[4] Sarkozy's point of view is apparently shared by the marketing team at *Le Monde*, the flagship of the French media, which on March 20, 2008 was offering a DVD set of "47 Oscar-winning films" as incentive to buy the paper at the newsstand. One is tempted by this to remember *Le Monde*'s famous headline immediately after 9/11 that "We are all Americans."

Deeper voices of European culture than Sarkozy, however, have shared Lang's anxiety despite their political pro-Americanism. Sir Isaiah Berlin, the late Oxford don and foremost historian of Western ideas was one.

Berlin was a champion of Johann Gottfried Herder's idea that each culture had a singular "volksgeist" that distinguished it from all others. For Herder the dignity of every person was tied up with the sense of belonging to that singular way of life. Herder had written that an outsider would not be able to grasp the masterpiece of a Scandinavian saga if he or she had not personally experienced a North Sea storm, an identity-forging event for those small cultures. Yet, if today's teenagers from Beijing to Moscow to Los Angeles can share the same thrill of Madonna either in concert or by satellite, what can the kind of cultural self-determination Lang and Berlin had in mind really mean?

Aware he was walking down the unfamiliar hallways of the approaching future, Berlin stood his ground.

"All the same," he responded,

> past differences take their toll: the spectacles through which the young of Bangkok or Valparaiso see Madonna are not the same. The many languages of the islands of Polynesia and Micronesia are said to be totally unlike each other; this is also true of the Caucasus.
>
> If you think that all this will one day give way to one universal language and culture – not just for learned purposes or politics or business, but to convey emotional nuances, to express inner lives – then I suppose what you suggest could happen. This would not be one culture; but the death of culture. I am glad to be as old as I am.[5]

Costa-Gavras, the Greek-French filmmaker who was so taken by American movies in his youth, is, like Lang and Berlin, similarly alarmed at Hollywood's inroads into other cultures. But, in the wake of the formation of the ABC-Disney mega-conglomerate back in 1995, he was also philosophical. "Anything so big and with so much power over the minds of men is dangerous to the democratic spirit. At the same time, as in Greece during the colonels," he said hopefully, referring to his film *Z*, "Goliaths necessarily call forth Davids."

Costa-Gavras understood how the dominant distribution system of American films stacked the deck. "When a big American film like *Jurassic Park* comes to Paris," he pointed out,

> the American distributors dictate the terms. They tell you "You can have *Jurassic Park* for 10 weeks, but to have it you must take another four or five American films to run along with it for two weeks each." This is called a train – a locomotive with cars following. Of course the exhibitor agrees because he won't be able to get another *Jurassic Park* to pull in the audiences. This means there is little room for French and other European titles in any given cinema.[6]

Not insignificantly, as we will discuss in a later chapter, this distribution equation is changing dramatically with DVDs and digital downloads outside the theater setting.

Sharing Costa-Gavras' concerns, in June 1998 the Canadian Minister of Cultural Heritage, Shelia Copps, convened a meeting of culture ministers from 20 countries in Ottawa with the stated aim of resisting America's media-industrial complex. She argued that "culture must be seen as more than merely entertainment ... in a world where information is power, the children of each community must have both the chance to hear the stories of their ancestors and make their own mark on the future of modern culture."[7] Ms. Copps told the other culture ministers that she was proud of the quotas which required 30 percent of what is played on English-speaking radio in Canada to be Canadian and 65 percent of the selection on French radio to be in the French language. She approvingly cited Mahatma Gandhi as saying "I do not want my house to be walled on all sides, and my windows to be stuffed. I want the cultures of all lands to blow about my house as freely as possible. But I refuse to be blown off my feet by any."

Shelia Copps, no longer a minister, successfully lobbied UNESCO to adopt a Cultural Diversity Convention to stop the onslaught of a global "mono-culture" which proclaims that any country has the right to exempt "cultural goods and services" from trade agreements. The convention was adopted by UNESCO in 2005 with a vote of 148–2. The US (and Israel) objected.

For some countries, the worry is not only that the dominance of American mass culture will eclipse its own, but that its damaging power to label others outstrips their own capacity to assert their identity.

Haluk Sahin is one of Turkey's top TV journalists. To this day, he is still steaming about "the unsolicited new identity" – "a media-age Star of David" – Turkey was branded with after the film *Midnight Express* portrayed his country as particularly brutal and intolerant. Worst of all, like most Turks, Sahin felt helpless to resist. "Great areas of the world, deeply rooted civilizations that have excelled in self-expression, have been rendered speechless in the new media order," he wrote in an exasperated essay entitled, "A Turkish Nightmare."[8] "Turkey may have the strongest army in the Middle East, but it has been proven powerless against a fictive attack far costlier than a bombing."

When David Puttnam produced this film, he thought he was making a socially-responsible statement about the degradation of the human spirit in conditions like that of a Turkish jail. He didn't imagine his film would be taken by local audiences as an indictment of their ancient, accomplished culture.

Along with the war in Iraq, this lasting bad taste about *Midnight Express* compounds the widespread anti-Americanism in that country today. The Turkish backlash has manifested itself precisely in cultural reassertion, using America as a foil. The most popular film in Istanbul in the spring of 2006 was entitled *The Valley of Wolves – Iraq*. Capturing the sentiments of ordinary Muslims throughout the region, it portrayed a Muslim Rambo who sets out on a mission of revenge against Americans in Iraq who are shown as looting and raping sadists.[9]

As Amar Bakshi of PostGlobal reported on his world trek, the most popular novel in Turkey in 2004 – selling 800,000 copies – was *Metal Firtina* (Metal Storm) by Burak Turna. The novel envisions a war between the US in 2007, which Turkey wins. The war begins in northern Iraq with hostilities instigated by an "evangelical president" of the US as a pretext to seize Turkey's rich deposits of uranium, thorium, and borax, and as part of the American plan for global domination.

In the popular novel, the US sets Turkey aflame and captures its capital, Ankara. Just as it threatens to divide the country among its Armenian and Greek neighbors, a powerful diplomatic alliance between Russia and the European Union comes to the rescue and stalls the US. Simultaneously, a Turkish agent smuggles a suitcase nuke through Mexico's border and detonates it in Washington, D.C. America falls to its knees. The war ends. Turkey, the good, prevails. America, the evil, loses.

Paradoxically – but hardly uniquely – this novel sprang from the imagination of a young writer weaned on American pop culture. Turna spent his childhood reading American comic books like *Mandrake the Magician* and watching *Star Wars, Star Trek, Indiana Jones*, and wild west movies.

Despite being steeped in American entertainment his whole life, what he calls "the will to power" posture and policies of the United States has turned him off, prompting him to look elsewhere for a model society and global leadership good for the Turks.[10]

Turna's latest novel is called *World War III* and envisions a shift of power away from the United States to Russia and China. "Even my mother knows this is going to happen," Turna said in January 2008 in Istanbul by way of explaining how this novel has also become a bestseller because it taps into a common sensibility shared today by the Turkish public.

In the metaphoric blender the occupation of Iraq against the will of the international community converges with the sense that America's presence is overbearing, even within the imaginative space of Turna's own culture guarded by the magnificent mosques of Turkey's own time of empire.

Modern Turkey has at least been linked to the West by the secular ideology of Ataturk, though that too is now under challenge by the governing Islamist-rooted Justice and Development Party which embodies the arrival of the once marginal Anatolian population at the center of power. As a political movement rooted in a conservative religious base, it may well object as much to the content and impulse of much of American mass culture as do others in the Muslim world, not to speak of the less enamored fans in the West itself.

"American film makers today have more freedom than any of their predecessors or peers," Martha Bayles has written. "Sometimes the results are wonderful. But sometimes they are deeply offensive: empty spectacle, sniggering adolescent treatments of sex and ultra-violent imagery. As a result, millions of foreigners feel assaulted. When Hollywood and Washington respond to their concerns by reducing film to the status of 'business, pure and simple,' they add insult to injury."[11] Many at home in the West feel assaulted as well by what Hollywood produces, starting with the revered pontiff of the world's billions of Catholics.

## Notes

1.  Gordon, M. "In Indonesia, Rumsfeld is Warned on U.S. Image." *New York Times*, June 6, 2006.
2.  Peres, S. and Pollack, S. "Out of Hollywood." *New Perspectives Quarterly* (Fall 1998) vol. 15, no. 5.
3.  Lang, J. "The Higher the Satellite the Lower the Culture." *New Perspectives Quarterly* (Fall 1991), vol. 8, no. 4.
4.  Sciolino, E. "French Youth at the Barricades, But a Revolution? It Can Wait." *New York Times*, March 28, 2006.
5.  "Two Concepts of Nationalism." Interview with Isaiah Berlin by Nathan Gardels, *New York Review of Books* (November 21, 1991), vol. 38, no. 19, p. 19.
6.  Gardels, N. (ed.) (1997) "Resisting the Colonels of Disney." Interview with Nathan Gardels in *The Changing Global Order* (Blackwell), p. 231.
7.  Copps, S. "Celine Dion: Made in Canada." *New Perspectives Quarterly* (Fall 1998), vol. 15, no. 5, p. 17.
8.  Sahin, H. "Midnight Express 20 Years Later." *New Perspectives Quarterly* (Fall 1998), vol. 15, no. 5, p. 21.

9. Ahmed, A. "From Media Mongols to Muslim Rambos." *New Perspectives Quarterly* (Spring 2006), vol. 23, no. 2, pp. 22–3.
10. Bakshi, A. C. (2007) "Metal Storm: Imagining U.S.-Turkey War." *PostGlobal.*
11. Bayles, M. "Risky Business for Hollywood." *International Herald Tribune*, May 8, 2008.

# Chapter 7

## Culture Wars in the West:
## The Pope vs. Madonna

One summer some years into his papacy, John Paul II gazed out from the terrace at Castel Gondolfo, the Pope's vacation residence outside of Rome, lost deep in contemplation and prayer. The global pastor was seeking guidance. Where could he have the greatest impact in saving the souls of men in his remaining time on earth?

He knew that Stalin, who once asked "How many divisions does the Pope have?" had been wrong in his sarcastic dismissal of the moral power of the church.

As he proved with his support of the rise of Solidarity, which was leading to the imminent demise of the Communist Party in his Polish homeland, the Pope indeed has many divisions. The soft power of believing hearts and minds could defeat the hard power of state repression.

Knocking down godless communism was no easy task, to be sure. The harder task by far, it occurred to the pontiff/ philosopher, was taking on what he saw as the impiety spreading across the secular West. Then it struck him. He had gone to the heart of the beast by returning home to celebrate mass outside of Warsaw and Krakow. If he wanted to grapple with the state of the soul in the West, he also had to go make his stand at the center of it all: Hollywood.

Foreshadowing the concerns of his successor, Pope Benedict XVI, John Paul II had come to believe that the "post-modern" values that so color the entertainment industry – the end of belief, the emergence of global secular culture, and the relativity of all values – were damaging his flock and said so in his encyclical, *The Splendor of Truth*.

So, in 1987 the traveling Pope headed to Universal Studios in Los Angeles to plead his case directly to the Hollywood executives.[1] When they gathered in the ballroom at the Sheraton Hotel, he did not make the mistake of underestimating Hollywood's soft power divisions the way the Communists had underestimated the church's.

"Filmmaker's power – for good and ill," he told the assembled crowd,

> is awesome. What you create not only reflects human society but also helps shape it. Hundreds of millions of people see your films and television programs, listen to your voices, sing your songs and reflect your opinions. It is a fact that your smallest decisions can have global impact. Rare is the priest, minister or rabbi, educator or politician who has the filmmaker's power to elevate or degrade the human person.

Many years later, during his first visit to the US in 2008, Pope Benedict XVI carried forward the worry that aggressive secularism reflected in the media was eroding the religious foundations of America. He told American bishops that "America's brand of secularism poses a particular problem. It allows for professing belief in God and respects the public role of religion, but at the same time can subtly reduce religious belief to the lowest common denominator. The result is a growing separation of faith from life."[2] For the present Pope excessive individualism and materialism separates the person from others and God. "If this seems counter-cultural," he said on his visit to the US, "that is simply further evidence of the urgent need for a renewed evangelization of culture." The culture wars which erupted within the West in the wake of the 1960s were played out, and continue to be played out, in the media and entertainment. The "Hollywood image" of the leader of the free world has generated doubts not only in many hearts and minds globally, but also at home.

The Pope's concerns are shared by many across the American spectrum.

As Martha Bayles notes,

> The 1980s and '90s were decades when many Americans expressed concern about the degradation of popular culture. Conservatives led campaigns against offensive song lyrics and Internet porn, liberal Democrats lobbied for a Federal Communications Commission crackdown on violent movies and racist video games; and millions of parents protected their kids from what they saw a socially irresponsible entertainment industry.[3]

To judge by a Pew Foundation Poll in April 2005, which Bayles cites, these worries have not abated. According to that poll "roughly six-in-ten Americans said they are very concerned over what children see or hear on TV (61 per cent); in music lyrics (61 per cent); in video games (60 per cent); and in movies (56 per cent)."

Indeed, Bill Bennett, Ronald Reagan's secretary of education, famously charged that Hollywood is undermining America's mainstream values. On the liberal side both Tipper Gore, as well as one of entertainment's own, Bill Cosby, have condemned the sexually explicit and misogynist lyrics in some strands of what they view as morally renegade rock and rap.

In their 2008 book *Come On People*, Cosby and Alvin Poussaint ask "What do record producers think when they churn out that gangsta rap with anti-social, women-hating messages? Do they think that black male youth won't act out what they have repeated since they were old enough to listen?"[4] Indeed, a Pew Poll in November 2007 indicated that 71 percent of blacks feel rap is a bad influence on their communities.

Especially after George W. Bush's second electoral victory secured by the support of the religious right, mostly liberal Hollywood is woefully aware of the "faith gap" that separates it from its audience. Hollywood executives say they would happily make 200 religious films a year if they thought they'd sell. This rings quite disingenuous since one of the highest grossing films of all time was Mel Gibson's *The Passion of the Christ* which he obstinately made in the face of widespread ridicule by the secular sophisticates who inhabit the Hollywood hills.

Though Sam Huntington's term "clash of civilizations" was meant to refer to the West's relationships with Confucian Asia and the theocratic proclivities of the Islamic world, arguably it applies in a way he didn't quite mean to the clash within the West itself. The clash is also between the Pope and Madonna, that is, between the postmodern dissing of all faith and authority from mom to imam on the one hand, and traditional religious culture on the other.

As if to make the point that American entertainment was driven only by "egoism" and "desire," Madonna staged her 2006 "Confessions" tour, in which she hung herself upside down on a cross, replete with a crown of thorns and a gaggle of leather-clad hunks dancing around her, practically on the doorstep of the Vatican. In a world torn by religious strife, this led to a rare joint condemnation of her act by Islamic, Jewish, and Christian leaders. No doubt they shared the sentiment of Tatyana Myasoyedova, who protested the concert when it came to Moscow. "The US first destroyed our country," she railed, "then they destroyed our economy. And now they send this horrible young woman to destroy our souls."[5]

The transformation of mass culture in America in the wake of the 1960s marked a point of departure from the days of the Eisenhower and *Leave It to Beaver* sensibility on which America's global appeal was largely based. This transformation occurred in movies, television and, especially, popular music.

Madeline Albright, the former US secretary of state, for one, is admirably humble on this subject, believing that America needs to be just as self-critical and possessed of humility with respect to its mass culture as it ought to be about episodes of misguided foreign policy like the war in Iraq. "I don't think we in America have yet fully understood the impact of the 1960s on how we view ourselves or how we are viewed by others, specifically the Islamic world, but also by mainstream religious figures like Pope John Paul II and now Pope Benedict."[6]

For better and worse, the arrival of the 1960s and the anti-Vietnam war movement altered the largely PG appeal of American mass culture. As the America iconified by Norman Rockwell gave way to the edgy influences of the counterculture on the mainstream, a new tension emerged both within America and with respect to the content of its influence globally.

It was in this period, as LA's Catholic Archbishop Roger Mahony said during Pope John Paul II's visit to Los Angeles, that entertainment began its evolution from the now unimaginable prohibition of the word "pregnant" when Lucy was expecting Little Ricky to permitting the use of almost any language or topic during the exploitative afternoon talk shows like the now defunct *Jenny Jones*, and the still running *Jerry Springer Show* that proliferated by the 1990s. Indeed, what studio today would even think of making a feature Hollywood film with major stars comfortably cast in a mainstream religious role as, for example, was the case in the 1948 classic *The Bishop's Wife* with David Niven, Cary Grant, and Loretta Young. Carl Bernstein of Watergate reporting fame labeled the America which emerged as "the talk show nation," arguing that "for the first time in our history, the weird and the stupid and the vulgar are becoming our cultural norm, even our cultural ideal."[7]

The issue is a lot deeper than trashy TV. It goes to the heart of the clash within the West and also between the West and Islam as a religious culture. That clash is about whether all values should be treated equally as a matter of choice, as if flipping from one channel to the next or deciding among an array of equal movie options at the cineplex. Indeed, the common refrain of the Hollywood mainstream to moral criticism has been to scream "choice" as a right of free society – that the parents ought to just turn off the set or avoid the movie theater if they don't like what they are seeing or their children are watching.

It is precisely this "whatever" ideology, however, that is the heart of the conflict of postmodern "anything goes for market share" entertainment values with both the more traditional Judeo-Christian values and a believing Muslim world. Pope Benedict believes this current is so strong he calls it "the dictatorship of relativism."[8] It is the instrument of the subtle erosion of faith he spoke about in his 2008 visit to the US.

Since culture, particularly the powerful mass culture of Hollywood, is the transmitter of the values a society holds we cannot speak in any meaningful way about the fusion, friction, and competition in the global public square without addressing this conundrum of choice within liberal civilization. There are no easy answers.

The late Isaiah Berlin famously made the distinction between "negative" and "positive" freedom – the first being "freedom from" tyranny and interference and the second being "freedom to" do what one will in his or her zone of non-interference; the freedom of self-realization.

Negative freedom has pretty much been accepted universally, in principle if not in practice, since the end of the Cold War. Even in China the zone of personal space has grown immensely.

But, almost by definition in a diverse world, positive freedom, the "freedom to," is not universal. Some people want to wear headscarves; others want to marry the same sex.

After the "end of history," when choice triumphed over repressive communist ideology, most conflicts are now precisely over the positive freedoms of lifestyle choices both promoted and reflected in the media.

Fukuyama, who famously professed the "end of history" idea, agrees:

> Most liberal democracies have been able to avoid this question of what positive freedoms they want to encourage because they haven't been challenged. Now they are challenged by minorities – Muslim immigrants in Europe, for example – or in some way by rising cultures in Asia that have a very strong sense of their own moral community, their own non-liberal values.

"In Europe especially," according to Fukuyama,

> the issue of immigration and identity converges with the larger problem of the valuelessness of post modernity. The rise of relativism has made it harder to assert positive values and therefore the shared beliefs Europeans demand of immigrants as conditions for citizenship. Postmodern elites have evolved beyond identities defined by religion and nation to what they regard as a superior place. But aside from their celebration of endless diversity and tolerance, they find it difficult to agree on the substance of the good life to which they aspire in common.

Though America is a far more religious society than Europe, the same relativist impulse permeates its entertainment culture.

For this reason, Fukuyama, like Albright, believes Americans ought to be a little more humble and self-critical since all the fruits of freedom are not necessarily appealing and can undermine as well as uplift character no matter what the box office appeal.

> America's seamier side is well known in the world. The image of America held by many critical Muslims, radical or otherwise, is not inaccurate. One of the delusions of American policy after 9/11 was to presume that if anti-Americanism was out there, it wasn't because of our policies or the Hollywood image but because we were misunderstood. That was a seductive impulse because it meant we wouldn't have to look inward and change ourselves or our policies.[9]

Clearly, the secular West, the values of which are carried by American mass culture globally, is having trouble figuring out which limits to erase versus where to draw boundaries.

The paradoxes of this predicament abound. Ayaan Hirsi Ali – the Somali immigrant, women's right activist, and author of *Infidel*, has fled from faith to reason in the name of freedom, defecting from the womb of Islam to become an "Enlightenment fundamentalist," as her detractors charge, and an atheist. Indeed, the French philosopher Bernard-Henri Levy has taken up the cause of demanding that the European Union provide for her personal security since she embodies the key idea of Europe – the universal freedom of reason. Her life has been at risk since Theo van Gogh, with whom she made a film critical of the treatment of women in Islamic cultures, was murdered in Amsterdam by a radical Islamist.

Yet, Europe's most famous secular liberal philosopher, Jürgen Habermas, now argues that since postmodern society is unable to generate its own values, it can only "nourish" itself from religious sources. For him, Western values – liberty, conscience, human rights – are grounded in the Judeo-Christian heritage.

According to Habermas, "unbridled subjectivity" – the relativism of personal choice as the criteria of belief which reigns today – clashes with "what is really absolute – the right of every creature to be respected as an 'image of God.'"

This problem of how secular and largely post-religious societies come up with values is critical as we move forward into the global glasshouse where the West, and America in particular, must compete globally for hearts and minds on an ever more level media playing field.

"The practical problem," as Fukuyama explains,

is whether you can generate a set of values that will politically serve the integrating liberal purposes you want. This is complicated because you want those values to be positive and mean something, but you also can't use them as the basis for exclusion of certain groups in society.

It is possible that we could succeed at doing one without the other. For example, the grounds of success of the American political experiment is that it has created a set of "positive" virtues that serve as the basis for national identity but are also accessible to people who are not white and Christian or in some way "blood and soil" related to Anglo-Saxon Protestant founders of the country.

These values are the content of the American Creed – belief in individualism, belief in work as a value, belief in the freedom of mobility and popular sovereignty.

Samuel Huntington calls these "Anglo-Protestant values," but at this point they have become de-racinated from these roots. You can believe them no matter who you are or where you came from. As kind of a practical solution to the positive value problem, it works pretty well. This kind of definition of the good life, I think, you can resolve without resolving the deeper philosophical issue.[10]

In this formulation, Fukuyama has hit on something critically important as we consider the content of American culture and its transmission globally. This practical American creed of a "geist" without a "volk" is really the core of America's unique appeal to the world. In essence it says to our competitors in the global battle for hearts and minds that, in a world of hybrid cultures, there is room for everything but the dream of purity. All fundamentalisms – class, race, or religion – are based on this deadly impulse to close off instead of open up, to exclude instead of embrace. In this respect the French philosopher Bernard-Henri Levy is right: "In the recent history of humanity, the hatred of America has been one of the main structural links among the three totalitarianisms – fascism, communism and Islamism."[11]

Inevitably, however, this embrace by the media of the "contamination" that comes along with cosmopolitanism will insult sensibilities and challenge beliefs when the boundaries of communities are crossed.

Certainly, one key lesson for the media-soaked West is that freedom of expression in an age when messages and images can be spread worldwide instantaneously cannot be protected just by some law on the books, but by a sense of propriety and responsibility among both the producers and consumers of culture.

In the words of Nobel laureate Wole Soyinka, a liberal world order cannot allow the forces of intolerance to define "the territory of insult,"[12] as they tried to do in the controversy over the Danish cartoons of the Prophet Mohammed. For Soyinka, the Prophet has no precedence over "the Muse of Irreverence" in free societies.

At the same time, responsible consumers of culture in turn have every right in a liberal order to condemn offense or stereotype or competitively project their own worldview – for example as Mel Gibson did when he financed, produced, and directed *The Passion of the Christ* as a counter-statement to secular Hollywood or indeed as does the vast, parallel cultural universe of televangelism and Christian publishing. What crosses the line is violence and intimidation, as was the case, for example, with Ayatollah Khomeini's fatwa against Salman Rushdie.

Liberal culture is necessarily a negotiation on a case by case basis involving issues of morality, taste, and perceptions of disrespect. But these must be its terms.

It is a big step forward just to understand that the clashes today within the West and between the West and the rest are in large measure about the contested cultural expressions of freedom. To preach, as George Bush did repeatedly throughout his disastrous tenure, that "freedom" is the answer to the world's woes is as lame and dangerous as the Salafist radicals proclaiming that "Islam is the answer" without distinguishing between the faith in one God and Taliban-style shari'a.

This deeper grasp of the forces behind the clash within the West itself affords an invaluable insight as well into the ferocity of the reaction among culturally conservative Islamists to the ways of the West. Terrorism is the bleeding edge of that clash.

## Notes

1.  http://www.lapdonline.org/history_of_the_lapd/content_basic_view/1131.
2.  Fisher, I. and Stolberg, S. G. "Pope Praises U.S., but Warns of Secular Challenges." *International Herald Tribune*, April 17, 2008.
3.  Bayles, M. "Goodwill Hunting." *Wilson Quarterly*, Summer 2005.
4.  Cosby, B. and Poussaint, A. (2007) *Come on People: On The Path from Victim to Victors.* Thomas Nelson Inc., p. 16.
5.  http://articles.latimes.com/2006/sep/11/world/fg-madonna11.

6.  "Religion and Culture Are Key Parts of 21st Century Foreign Policy."
    Interview with Nathan Gardels for *Global Viewpoint*, syndicated by
    Tribune Media Servcies Intl., May 8, 2006.
7.  Bernstein, C. "Unlike Watergate, This is National Madness." *New
    Perspectives Quarterly* (Fall 1998), vol. 15, no. 5, p. 39.
8.  Dionne, E. J. "Cardinal Ratzinger's Challenge." *Washington Post*,
    April 19, 2005.
9.  "The Challenge of Positive Freedom." Interview with Nathan
    Gardels. *New Perspectives Quarterly* (Spring 2007), vol. 24, no. 2,
    pp. 53–6.
10. "The Challenge of Positive Freedom." Interview with Nathan
    Gardels. *New Perspectives Quarterly* (Spring 2007), vol. 24, no. 2,
    pp. 53–6.
11. "Anti-Americanism in the Old Europe." Interview with Nathan
    Gardels. *New Perspectives Quarterly* (Spring 2003), vol. 20, no. 2,
    pp. 5–11.
12. Soyinka, W. "Psychopaths of Faith vs. the Muse of Irreverence." *New
    Perspectives Quarterly* (Spring 2006), vol. 23, no. 2, p. 12.

# chapter 8

# Media Storm Troopers of the West vs. Islam

L ong before Osama bin Laden conceived of the assault on the Twin Towers in New York, Akbar Ahmed, a Pakistani scholar and former ambassador to Great Britain, sensed the mentality of siege gripping the Islamic world. For Ahmed, Hollywood films, CNN, and MTV have been the "storm troopers" of the West in the eyes of many Muslims. "The age of the media in Muslim society has dawned," he wrote in 1986,[1] after an extended trip through the remote villages of the Pakistan–Afghan frontier where the Taliban got its start.

> Muslims need to face up to the fact that there is no escape now, no retreat, no hiding place, from the demon. The more traditional a religious culture in our age of the media, the greater the pressure upon it to yield. Beneath layers of nuance, the collision between the global civilization emanating from the West and Islam is a straight out fight between two approaches to the world, two philosophies. One is based on secular materialism, the other in faith; one has rejected belief altogether; the other has placed it at the center of its world-view.

"Muslim parents," Ahmed continued, "blanch at the Western media because of the universality, power and pervasiveness of their subversive images, and because of their malignity and hostility toward Islam.… the videos that accompany pop songs produce ever more bizarre images from Madonna masturbating to Michael Jackson transmogrifying into a panther."

Akbar imagined that "it must have been something like this in 1258 when the Mongols were gathering outside Baghdad to shatter forever the greatest Arab empire in history. But, this time, the decision will be final. If Islam is conquered, there will be no coming back."

In many ways, Akbar's observations here, though descriptive, echo the now famous reflections of Sayyid Qutb, the Salafist militant who inspired Osama bin Laden and his followers, about the sinfulness and decadence of the West he experienced during his visit to the United States in 1948. They demonstrate the continuing preoccupation of Muslims troubled by the encroaching cultural influence of the powerful American superpower over the hearts and minds of the *ummah*.

Some typical excerpts from Qutb's notes tell the whole story. For him, America seemed "a reckless, deluded herd that only knows lust and money." Like many radical Islamists today, he was obsessed with sex and the freedom of women: "A girl looks at you, appearing as if she were an enchanting nymph or an escaped mermaid, but as she approaches, you sense only the screaming instinct inside her, and you can smell her burning body, not the scent of perfume but flesh, only flesh. Tasty flesh, truly, but flesh nonetheless."[2]

Akbar Ahmed is slightly less alarmed about total domination today since there has been an explosion of Muslim media, particularly in the Arab world, from Al Jazeera to the Dubai Film Festival to a proliferation of websites, unfortunately including jihadist websites that directly promote terrorism. There are more than 200 pan-Arab satellite channels. Yet, the core of his concern remains – a culture war in which Western news and the secular liberal entertainment media clash aggressively with Islamic notions of piety as well as a festering resentment over humiliation at the hands of the West perpetually exemplified by what they see as the unjust occupation of Palestine.

Ahmed's view is shared to some extent by Francis Fukuyama, who sees the global clash as an extension of America's own culture wars. "There has been a culture war going on within the United States for a long time," Fukuyama says. "Cultural conservatives and the religious right have long criticized Hollywood for undermining the values of family and faith. In a sense, their position is not all that different from Osama bin Laden's. The valuelessness projected by American mass culture *is* a problem."[3]

"Obviously," Fukuyama hastened to add, "Muslim extremists don't accept the basic framework of liberal tolerance within which America's culture wars are waged. but there is a relationship. What we see today on a global stage is in some sense an extension of America's own culture wars."

Zbigniew Brzezinski, the hard-nosed national security adviser to Jimmy Carter when he was president, shares Fukuyama's insight, perhaps because he is a conservative Roman Catholic. American culture, Brzezinski believes, has become a "permissive cornucopia," undermining America's capacity to be a systemic model for others. "Americans must face the fact that our own mass culture intensifies cultural cleavages around the world," he says. "Otherwise we are in no position to criticize other cultures for their religious principles concerning relations between the sexes."[4]

Perhaps the most difficult issue to ferret out is the extent to which the American media message can be liberating versus the extent to which its inspires reactionary and defensive responses that evolve into political challenges. This is a new post-post-Cold War conundrum for America and the West in general for which history offers no precedent.

Like its philosophical cousin, Marxism, liberalism assumed its universality. We assumed that our definition of the "good life" was shared by all if only the priests, autocrats, commissars, and strongmen would get out of the way. That some might not embrace extremism in the name of liberty, indeed might even prefer order and authority, or might one day have the clout to reject our secular and libertarian premises, certainly did not occur to us in the triumphant days after the Cold War. Like Marxism, in this sense we had no political theory of how to deal with cultural pluralism.

Since culture is not static, its evolution, its constant clashes and fusions, are not easily subject to measurement. We can however examine a few cases that clearly illustrate the double edge quality of America's mass cultural influence on the world, particularly the Muslim world.

## Stepping Outside the Frame

The futurist Alvin Toffler, a film buff who invented the term "future shock," once said that the power of movies or television shows is that they can transport you to an alternative reality without any of the associated risks, dislocations, and insecurities that always accompany change. The media sociologist, Manuel Castells, sees the same power to transport as Toffler does, but gives more weight to its impact.

For Castells, venturing into another reality through movies or other image media, or even the "imaginative knowledge" of literature, is not cost free. Glimpsing an alternative reality can either prompt innovation – "I want to live that way" – or provoke reaction – "that way of living is dangerous and a threat to my way of life." Surely, this insight accounts for the strange and elusive mixture of love and loathing American mass culture evokes around the globe.

**Plate 1**   John Wayne holding a gun in *Stage Coach*. Reproduced by permission of United Artists Entertainment

**Plate 2**   Iwo Jima flag being raised for *Letters from Iwo Jima*. Reproduced by permission of Paramount Pictures

**Plate 3** *The Spy Who Came in from the Cold.* Reproduced by permission of Paramount Pictures

**Plate 4** *Pirates of the Caribbean: Dead Man's Chest*, dir. Gore Verbinski, copyright © 2006. Reproduced by permission of The Walt Disney Company

**Plate 5** Kid shooting at the bus in the movie *Babel*, dir. Alejandro González Iñárritu, copyright © 2006. Reproduced by permission of Paramount Pictures

**Plate 6**  Scene from *Crouching Tiger, Hidden Dragon*, dir. Ang Lee, copyright © 2003. Appears courtesy of Sony Pictures Classics Inc.

As an illustration of how the prism of American popular culture refracts differently for different people, we draw on discussions with four women to assess the impact on hearts and minds. These women are Ayaan Hirsi Ali, author of *Infidel*, a memoir of her defection from Islam; Masoumeh Ebtekar, a one-time student radical who rose to become the highest-ranking woman in the Iranian government; Benazir Bhutto, two-time prime minister of Pakistan who was assassinated in 2007; and Madeleine Albright, a former United States secretary of state. To sum up, we include the reflections of Haris Silazdjic, the prime minister of Bosnia during the war, about how images can frustrate as much as elevate people in societies going through wrenching transitions.

## From Secret Admirer to Infidel

"If you go to the 'house of the devil' you will lose your soul and bring calamity on your life." That is what Ayaan Hirsi Ali's grandmother, an illiterate Somali nomad caring for Ayaan and her sister in Nairobi, warned ominously. One hot and interminably boring day in 1984, however, Ayaan, then 15, and her sister couldn't contain their youthful restlessness and gave in to temptation. Instead of studying the Koran as their grandmother told them to do when she went out for the day, they donned their headscarves and stealthily negotiated Nairobi's back alleys to the movie house.

Here, for the first time in their lives, they saw something shocking: a boy and girl kiss in public on the screen as naturally and openly as if they were peeling sweet potatoes preparing dinner at home. The movie they saw, *Secret Admirer* – incidentally produced by one of the authors – was a thoroughly immemorable Hollywood farce for those who saw it in America, but it changed their lives. What was this other planet where people lived this way? The America presented on the screen offered an alternative reality they, out of their own experience, could have never imagined.

As the floodgates came down and televisions spread through Hirsi Ali's neighborhood, more and more kids watched American TV programs, inviting the devil into their own house. Hirsi Ali particularly remembers *Diff'rent Strokes*, the sitcom with Gary Coleman living with a white family.

In a way, Hirsi Ali's grandmother was right. Along with other far more critical experiences – from having her clitoris "cut" at an early age to an arranged marriage – the path on which this young Somali girl embarked that day by being exposed to a silly Hollywood film led years later to her avowed atheism and confrontation with traditional Islam and the Muslim shari'a code, which Hirsi Ali today regards as "elevated tribal law."

As she recounts in her memoir, *Infidel*, calamity indeed came upon her life when, after migration to the Netherlands, she scripted her own film, *Submission*, about the ill treatment of women in Islamic cultures. The filmmaker, Theo van Gogh, an avant-garde cinemetic provocateur and great-grandnephew of the famous Dutch painter, was murdered for his efforts by a radical Islamist on the streets of Amsterdam. Van Gogh's throat was slit, and anchored to his chest with the knife was a note saying Ayaan Hirsi Ali was next.

Hirsi Ali now lives in the United States and is trying to organize her own security since the government of Holland will only provide it when she is on their soil, which, of course, is the very place where she is most in danger. But because she stands defiantly at the nexus of the conflict between the West and radical Islam – the role of women – she, surely correctly, feels threatened everywhere.

Having experienced the power of cinema in her own life, she is now also determined to convince Hollywood that it should stop "neglecting its responsibility" and focus its talents on helping lift Muslim women, especially those in Africa and the Arab world, where tribal norms still rule, out of their oppressive lives by showing them how, as in other societies, modern women can be free and live with dignity.

## From the Shah to the Spice Girls

Growing up in the Shah's Iran, Masoumeh Ebtekar was a serious and pious girl, put off by what she saw as the decadence and corruption of the modernizing regime allied with the United States. Rather than being attracted to the West by what she saw at the movies or heard when listening to rock n' roll, she was repelled. As the Shah's repression deepened and Iran became ever more Westernized, she became a dedicated revolutionary. Unlike many other teenage girls, she idolized Ayatollah Khomeini, not Michael Jackson.

When the Shah fled in 1979 and Khomeini returned from exile, she was not only among the students who seized the American embassy and held the diplomats hostage but was their spokesperson. Her agitated daily proclamations from the embassy compound proved the prelude to a purge of all secular and moderate voices from the revolution to make way for an Islamic theocracy ruled by shari'a.

A little more than two decades later, Ebtekar had risen to the post of vice president and environment minister in the reformist government of Mohammad Khatami, making her the highest-ranking woman in Iran. It was then, back in 1998, that she agreed to talk with us as part of the now abandoned "dialogue of civilizations" initiated by Khatami to define the terms of Iran's future relations with the West.

Draped in a black chadoor from head to toe, she pointedly recoiled at the offer to shake hands with a man when we met.

The key question was obvious: A real dialogue between civilizations wouldn't mean sitting down with Samuel Huntington in some academic seminar room. It would mean addressing how the revolution which overthrew the Shah now proposed to deal with MTV and the heavy metal music said to be most popular among teenagers who listen in darkened rooms while the guardians of virtue roam outside. "The doors of the world today are wide open, whether we like it or not. Our youth, like those of other societies, are attracted to the seeming glamour of this entertainment culture," she readily admitted. "Aren't we allowed to have any fun in an Islamic society?" this proponent of Islamic feminism says she is constantly asked. "Is Islam a religion that prohibits everyone from enjoying life? Undeniably, it is a challenge to the Islamic revolution to find another model of enjoyment and fulfillment than the casual, carefree, sensate lifestyle Hollywood, to use the catch phrase, promotes as universal."

In Ebtekar's worldview, it is a matter of cultural diversity.

> Must we all conform to Hollywood's view of human nature, which mostly stresses what is base rather than noble in humanity? What about human dignity, particularly the portrayal of women as little more than sex objects? Isn't there something more to existence than consumer status and a few moments of pleasure in a life that is otherwise empty and meaningless? I think the basic legacy of the postmodernist, consumer culture of the West is to enjoy life for the moment at the expense of not thinking about the rest of society or the future of the world, as if somehow it is possible just to take a perpetual vacation from reality. Essentially it is living without responsibility. The greatest tragedy of our time is carried within this Hollywood culture: life deprived of a spiritual dimension.

Recalling her militant days holding hostages at the American embassy, for which she doesn't apologize, Ebtekar updated the tasks of the revolution. "My generation faced political and military domination by the West. We had to deal with the Shah. The younger generation must face the Spice Girls. Today, the West doesn't have to deploy its armies and naval fleets, only its satellites and TV broadcasts. That is even a deeper threat to Islam."

By 2005, the reformist government in which Ebtekar so prominently served lost out to even more radical theocrats led by Mahmoud Ahmadinejad, who became president. By 2006, Ebtekar and other reformists were back, sweeping the local elections in Tehran and elsewhere in a sign of dissatisfaction over Ahmadinejad's poor performance, squandering his efforts denying the Holocaust instead of creating jobs.

The fact that Masoumeh Ebtekar is a top reformer in the Iranian context only underscores the cultural distance between Islamic believers and the West.

In next-door Iraq, there are many who are also not buying what the US is selling from a cultural standpoint. Indeed, one wonders what the Grand Ayatollah Ali-al Sistani, the Shiite leader to whom the US has handed over Iraq through democratic elections, would have thought had he watched Janet Jackson during the half time show at the Super Bowl a few years ago. As he sat stroking his long white beard in his sparse room at the Najaf seminary, he no doubt would have mused it was bad enough that France, the birthplace of the secular West, banned the headscarf for Muslim girls. Worse, the ayatollah surely told himself, there is an inexorable continuum from that imposition of immodesty to Janet Jackson bearing her breast before tens of millions of viewers. Is this what we want for our Islamic democracy? he might well have asked. No doubt, he would direct anyone who wants an answer to that question to his website, www.sistani.org, which begins with a stream of blessings upon the wronged, including, "Salutations upon the pure women who were paraded without their veils." It also dispenses advice to the faithful, as when a young man from the United Arab Emirates was told "no", it was not moral to play the guitar.[5]

## The Taliban and Desperate Housewives

Since 9/11, the nominal bridge between the West and Islam was supposed to be Pakistan. But the chasm there has grown ever greater. Another woman, the most thoroughly Westernized of any leader of a Muslim country, offered some insights about why this is the case.

Benazir Bhutto, assassinated while campaigning for the return of democracy in late 2007, tried holding the line against reactionary Islamists during her two terms as prime minister of Pakistan – including against her own intelligence services which were scheming successfully to install the Taliban in power in neighboring Afghanistan. When she was in exile, she discussed the impact of American mass culture on her own people – now aligned, if through a dictatorship, with the US in the war on terror – during a visit to her cousin's house in the smoggy hills above Pomona, California.

> Within the Muslim world, the word sex is not used. Sex is not discussed. There is a reaction, therefore, against the sexual overtones that come across in American mass culture from music to films and TV programs. Look at *Desperate House-wives*, just to take one example. In societies which are not literate and largely tribal, America is viewed through such a prism as an immoral society.

"The clash in the Muslim world today," she continued, adjusting her headscarf, "is between those who want material success and those who pursue spiritual success. Those who want material success want to join the global march. The militants say 'No, you shouldn't want to make money and live the good life. You should want the simple life as lived in the early days of Islam.' "

The militants, says Bhutto, exploit this tension to make people feel they are selling out Islam if they are sympathetic to the West. "They make use of the overly sexual, some say decadent, society projected by the Western media and say that to join globalization is to become corrupted spiritually. This is despite the fact that, Hollywood images aside, most Americans are very religious."

Tragically, Bhutto understood the situation all too well. When she was assassinated in December 2007, the Pakistani government fingered the chief plotter as Baitullah Masud, who is closely linked Maulana Qazi Fazlullah known locally in the tribal zone of South Waziristan as the "FM mullah." He extols his radicalized flock to condemn the education of girls and resist contamination of Western culture by burning their TV sets. In God's eyes, he told his followers, "burning a TV set is worth killing three Jews."[6]

## Offended in Kansas as Well as Karachi

Perhaps because she was not only the first woman, but also the first mother, to become US secretary of state, Madeleine Albright looks at the world much differently than her predecessors. For Albright international affairs are not just about official treaties or the size of armed forces, but about culture, lifestyle, and religious commitments. She spoke with us in March 2006 about Hollywood, the '60s, parents, and Islam.

Certainly, the whole '60s ethos has had a big impact on how the conservative, traditional Islamic world looks at America.

There is no question. The face we show is one of great permissiveness. Women go around with their midriffs exposed, or worse. I have to tell you, I'm horrified whenever I watch some American television shows when they appear on the screen in Istanbul or Cairo. What must these people think about America? That really has undermined our ability to present ourselves as a role model.

The problem is that modernization, like globalization, is not something you can stop. You have to figure out how to mitigate the worst parts of it. We are having a very hard time doing that at the moment because we are not in a position to promote what's good because so much of the negative is out there.

I can totally understand that people in Karachi can be offended by the excesses of American mass culture, because they are in Kansas, too. There is a reaction to the over-permissiveness we see in our culture. I feel like an old fuddy-duddy saying this, but I understand this perfectly. I raised a family and can't tell you how many times I had to turn the TV off or change the channel when my girls were growing up.

Part of what has happened is that certain aspects of America that people saw when they used to watch shows like *Dallas* or *Dynasty* became part of the global revolution of rising expectations. The prosperity portrayed in these TV dramas created both a desire to be like that, but also envy at not being like that. It made clear the divide between the rich and the poor world.

Now, we have something different – the violence, the sex and vulgarity. That is something that offends people; they don't want to be that way. This is the kind of society they don't want.

What can we do about it, we asked the former secretary of state? "We can't be in favor of censorship," she acknowledged.

What we're left with is a plea to the creators of entertainment to develop a sense of propriety. They must have a sense of civic responsibility – only with a global scope because that is the world we live in today.

The Danish cartoon episode was an example of this. No one in the West could say flat-out that those depictions of the prophet should not have been published. But what one has to do is realize there needs to be propriety and responsibility if you are going to live in a society where your freedom of expression is protected.

What we need to understand, above all, is that we now live in an age of information technology by which anything can be spread. Religion can be spread that way, too. In fact, we see it with the televangelists. Some help spread a message of hope, love, unity, tolerance and responsibility. Others spread a message of hate and division, us versus them. This is part of the prism today in which politics and international relations have to be seen. You can't ignore it because the media ties us all together.

## The Age of Non-Information

Perhaps the most trenchant analysis of the challenges to Islam in the information age was offered by Haris Silajdzic. The prime minister of Bosnia from 1992–5, Silajdzic received his Koranic education in Libya. His father headed the largest mosque in Sarajevo.

Bosnia, like Iran, Egypt, Malaysia, and Pakistan are all trying to step into modernity, as he sees it:

While the revolutions of literacy, telecommunications and travel have exposed ordinary Muslims to the glamorous material symbols of modernity, such a reality remains beyond the reach of all but one or two percent of the population. So there is frustration and anger. To fill this gap between dreams and reality people cling to what they trust, their cultural identity and their religion. As a religion, Islam is especially comforting because it is comprehensive. It provides answers for all situations in life, including an answer to the spiritual vacuum of the West.[7]

It disturbs Silajdzic that this return to the comforts of faith is seen as "fundamentalism" in the West:

> Like the Muslims of the East, the heads of Westerners these days are so overloaded with information they can only organize their world with labels and by resorting to prejudice.
>
> Images of distant places are taken for reality. Whether looking East to West or vice-versa, grasping complexity seems a luxury our fast-paced times can no longer afford. The rush of the media is bringing people together as never before, but people are not ready. Man's nature is incremental. He needs time to absorb change and adapt, to acculturate. Information can be helpful, but it can also be dangerous if the speed of the deluge only creates false ideas, anxiety and suspicion.

With the arrival of a truly multipolar world, culturally as well as politically and economically, a vast pluralism of storytelling will explode. The question is whether we will catch only sound bites or video clips through our fragmented platforms, as Silajdzic fears, or whether we will really listen to and understand the stories of others?

## Notes

1. Ahmed, A. (1995) "Media Mongols at the Gates of Baghdad," in N. Gardels (ed.), *At Century's End.* Alti, pp. 22–4.
2. Wright, L. (2006) *The Looming Tower: Al-Qaeda and the Road to 9/11.* Alfred A. Knopf, pp. 11–12.
3. "The Challenge of Positive Freedom." Interview with Nathan Gardels. *New Perspectives Quarterly* (Spring 2007), vol. 24, no. 2, pp. 53–6.

4. "Hostility to America Has Never Been Greater." Interview with Nathan Gardels. *New Perspectives Quarterly* (Summer 2004), vol. 21, no. 3, pp. 5–9.
5. Sistani, A. A. (2005) Sistani.org: The Official Website of Grand Ayatollah Sistani; "When Janet Jackson Meets Ayatollah Ali al-Sistani." *New Perspectives Quarterly* (Spring 2004), vol. 21, no. 2, pp. 2–4.
6. Ali, Z. and King, L. "Pakistan Signs Truce with Militant Faction." *Los Angeles Times*, May 22, 2008.
7. Silajdzic, H. (1997) "Islam: Postman of Civilization," in N. Gardels (ed.), *The Changing Global Order*. Blackwell, pp. 44–5.

# Chapter 9

# New Stories, New Audiences in the Global Age

The cellist Yo-Yo Ma, famous for his Silk Road Project which promotes artistic exchanges along the old trading route which once connected the world, looks at the future of the globalization of culture by looking back. For Yo-Yo Ma, culture is a "fabric" woven from many strands coming from past history as well as from every corner of the world. "At the core of any cellist's repertoire are the Cello Suites by Bach," he explains,

> and at the heart of each suite is a dance movement called the sarabande. This dance originated with music of the North Africa Berbers, where it was a slow, sensual dance. It next appeared in Spain, where it was banned because it was considered lewd and lascivious. Spaniards brought it to the Americas, but it also traveled to France where it became a courtly dance. In the 1720s, Bach incorporated the sarabande into his Cello Suites. Today, I play Bach, a Paris-born American musician of Chinese heritage.[1]

Globalization this time around will also produce a new mix of cultural influences through the art forms and media of our age – not only through music and the fine arts, but through web series, video games, television, and movies as well. There will be many combinations of influence, from the growing presence of Indian and Chinese films in the West to the ever more popular spread of Latin telenovelas to the growing cultural autonomy of the indigenous silver screen everywhere, from joint-productions across the world by giants such as Disney to the hopeful emergence of a new global cinema.

In short, in the realm of media and entertainment we are already seeing the corollary of "the rise of rest" Fareed Zakaria and Parag Khanna have described in the realm of politics and economics, including a greater presence in the West of non-Hollywood product and greater cultural competition in markets previously dominated by Hollywood.

In October, 2008 Vladmir Putin promised $76 million to the Russian film industry for "films aimed at creating a system of values corresponding to the interests of Russian society and the strategic goals of national development." A burst of Indian films, such as *Monsoon Wedding* and even some Bollywood musicals have dazzled audiences in the West. *Crouching Tiger, Hidden Dragon*, the Ang Lee film, is the highest-grossing non-English film of all time.[2]

This same phenomenon can be seen in TV. For years the most popular TV show in the world has been *The Bold and the Beautiful*, an American production which had 500 million viewers in 98 countries as late as the year 2000. Today *The Simpsons*, according to the *Hollywood Reporter*, "is quite possibly the biggest international TV hit of all time. Multiple generations of fans in the millions tune in to the series each day overseas; statistics show that about 50 million viewers watch the animated sitcom each week. In all, the series is airing in more than 100 countries."[3]

These days, however, they share the small screens everywhere with Latin American telenovelas that have a 2-billion-strong audience in 100 countries, including Russia and China.[4]

Telenovelas are produced in Venezuela, Brazil, and Colombia, but the true font of the genre is Mexico City. "With telenovelas, you've got a universal product, laughs and tears, at a very good price," Martìn Luna Ortigoza, production chief for TV Azteca, the second-largest producer of telenovelas, told the *Arizona Republic*.[5]

The shows seem to transcend political divisions as well, with audiences in Israel and its Arab neighbors enjoying the same series. In conservative Muslim countries, Marcel Vinay, TV Azteca's vice president of international sales notes, scripts are tweaked and footage edited to eliminate kissing or explain away out-of-wedlock pregnancies. In Israel, the translators gloss over Catholic phrases and concepts.

According to Luna Ortigoza, telenovela sales are increasing at 25 percent a year, with Eastern Europe growing the fastest. Televisa, the number one telenovela studio and producer of such hits as *Rubi* and *Woman of Wood*, has launched websites in Russian and English for fans.[6]

Already back during the first democratic election in Russia after the fall of the Soviet Union in the '90s, a journalist went to interview Gennady Zhuganov, the head of the rump Communist Party. Waiting in the outer office, he witnessed the party head's secretaries giddily enthralled by their daily Mexican soap opera, Russian subtitles running along the bottom of the screen.

Increasingly, as melodramatic as they intentionally are, telenovelas are rapidly becoming a cultural force. When one Brazilian show named *Family Ties* dealt with a character that needed a bone marrow transplant after contracting leukemia, public opinion toward organ donation completely changed, according to the BBC.

While the main telenovela producers in Mexico and Brazil have often been criticized for being too closely aligned with the political powers of the moment and not allowing any criticism of the government, that is now changing, according to TV Azteca's Maria Luisa Alves.

"More controversial events are being included in the Mexican telenovela," she says. "They have featured homosexuality, having a child with special needs, abortion, and sex before marriage. In a very Catholic society, I think that is a lot to say on public television at prime time."[7]

In some countries, American content on TV and in music has diminished greatly. In South Korea, for example, 92 percent of TV and video games are domestically produced. In Spain in 2000, 60 percent of the total $1 billion in music sales were generated by Spanish and Latin American artists – though *The Simpsons* is aired several times a week.

Global content is also finding its way back to the US. *Ugly Betty*, originally a Colombian soap opera, has Mexican and American clones, suitably adjusted. And that is but one example, along with shows like *The Office*, of how Hollywood has adapted "scripted foreign formats" for broadcast in America and in order to make contact with new ideas that can also be re-exported. "We're opening our doors to the entire world," says Ben Silverman, co-chairman of NBC Entertainment and Universal Media Studios.

> We're not just looking to one place for those ideas. I want to bring an entrepreneurial energy to our broadcast channel and work with foreign partners because the foreign marketplace is incredibly rich right now, and if we can come up with ideas that sell globally from the beginning, like *Heroes*, it benefits how you finance them.[8]

As the *Los Angeles Times* pointed out in reporting on this trend, "this kind of creative exchange works both ways and is hard evidence of a shrinking global entertainment world."[9] Just as Hollywood looks around for new influences its own influence remains considerable. Many of the most popular shows in America are also hits around the world – including *CSI: Miami*, *Lost*, and *Heroes* among them.

This two-way trend will surely accelerate as the digital production and distribution revolution empowers all cultures, and even individuals, to contend in the global public square.

The proliferation of platforms globally has created vast new media opportunities. The "flatness of the world" caused by the spreading digital consumer economy means, by Viacom chief Sumner Redstone's surmise, that "increasingly, global media distribution is a two-way tidal wave."[10] American programming is flowing overseas, as before, but increasingly indigenous programming abroad is being financed by visionary companies like Viacom or Disney who seek to become a local instead of a foreign brand.

More than half of Viacom's on-line audience lies outside the United States. Localized MTVs create their own programming across 142 TV channels, almost 300 websites, and 35 mobile TV channels. Viacom has just launched MTV Arabia, soon to be followed by Nickelodeon – all suitably wrestling with controversies ranging from how to portray unmarried boys and girls mingling to coping with any offensive lyrics from whatever American hip hop goes into the mix.

In his remarks to the Nielsen Media & Money Conference in New York at the end of 2007, Redstone offered several salient insights into how technological advance is spawning new stories and new audiences.

First, Redstone argued that "content" is still king. No matter what the media platform, entertainment

thrives on good old-fashioned story telling. Control of the media experience has been migrating toward the consumer for years, but the scales have now tipped and the consumer has taken charge.... there is no going back. Our days of broadcasting to a captive audience are gone. The combination of broadband speeds, desegregation, the rise of digital social networking and the power of search favors content that is vital, ubiquitous and easy to use.[11]

For Redstone, the new media model is clear: "move the mountain to Mohammed," that is, bring the content the consumer wants to whatever platform he or she has chosen. The vast new opportunities lie in "taking us with them wherever they go."

"The more platforms our content is on," in Redstone's considered view – with mobile devices as the next prime-time-all-the-time venue – "the more numerous the revenue streams. And with 500 channels and 8 billion Internet sites out there, digital means dollars for those with the best content."

"Viacom," says Redstone "is the biggest producer of mobile content in the world. We are locked on young, edgy, clippable comedy and music content. ... all the snackable stuff that multi-tasking, wireless demographics love." As Redstone and others follow where the market takes them, the "adolescizing of culture" that Sydney Pollack worried about seems to be accelerating.

Where Redstone sees dollar signs others see diversity. A pink bungalow at the Beverly Hills Hotel near where starlets famously lazed around the palm fringed pool was an unlikely place to find the Muslim prime minister of Malaysia. But that is where Mohammed Mahathir, Asia's best known bête noire of liberal America along with his authoritarian neighbor to the south, Singapore's Lee Kuan Yew, had come to drum up business in Hollywood.

Co-author of the defiant tome *An Asia That Can Say No* with the Japanese nationalist Shintaro Ishihara, the then-Malaysian premier was looking for investors in his "multimedia super corridor," which he hoped would catapult his small nation into a tropical hub of the information age. Laced with his vision of how the information age would unfold was not so much anti-Americanism as confidence in Asia's rising future.

Anticipating the changes now underway back in the 1990s, Mahathir lamented then that

> entertainment is almost entirely American in its cultural content. The characters are American, their problems are American, and their dialogue is American. Most of the rest of the world experiences this at a superficial level. Because of the glitz and special effects, that may be enough for now. That is why action movies are the most popular outside America.
>
> But technology will make these advantages disappear. Digital entertainment based on action and special effects can be developed anywhere. Digital action heroes will become more and more realistic.[12]

By 2006, indeed, South Korea and Japan were already the masters of digital animation movies.

Mahathir goes on to say:

> This reality converges with another. As developing countries get richer, they will want more local content for their entertainment. Themes may be universal, but Asians will increasingly prefer entertainment that is localized in its languages, myths, music and characters. We are already seeing this in television; sooner or later the same trend will be true in movies and computer games.
>
> People everywhere want, first of all, to link their entertainment with their own material aspirations. As they become secure through their success, they will look for deeper fulfillment. They want to improve themselves, to be touched by something more than materialism or escapism.
>
> This is the realm of religion, culture and moral values which requires a context that goes well beyond America's pop

culture. In Asia, the major cultures are Confucianism, Islam and Hinduism, each with a rich history that are a deep source of creative content.[13]

Thanks to the rise of the rest which challenges not only America's dominance, but its presence, Mahathir's thesis is being tested. An illustrative survey of China, India, and the Arab world reveals both the conflict and convergences as the global media landscape undergoes transformation.

Post-Mao China's leaders have grasped the power of television in their vast land as a means to support their vision of market reform and opening up. By 1987, as Deng Xiaoping's reforms began to kick in, Hu Qili, the Party ideology chief at the time, approved the airing of *Yellow River Elegy* – a TV show which promoted the idea that China would prosper from looking outward instead of inward, across the sea instead of to the Yellow River.

More recently in 2007 Chinese TV broadcast a long historical series called *The Rise of Great Nations* as a kind of lesson to Chinese viewers about how a nation can become a great power. Included among the lessons was Britain's rise, which the show attributed, remarkably for state television, to the Magna Carta and the divestiture of the "divine right" of kings by an elected parliament![14]

New York University professor Ying Zhu has followed television-watching patterns in China for some years, noting that prime time programming at the turn of the decade was dominated by Qing Dynasty dramas – just of the kind Mahathir projected – first focusing on corruption and cultural decline and then later on the prosperity and national unity associated with the early Qing period.

Yang notes the metaphoric crossover between the image media and politics, suggesting that the popular 1999 TV series *Yongzsheng Dynasty* "reminded the Chinese of their former premier Zhu Rongji" who was acclaimed for his anti-corruption campaigns under President and party leader Jiang Zemin. Zhu himself was said to be a big fan of the show.[15]

Tracing the rise of the new Chinese dream of social mobility and opportunity is a version of *American Idol*. Called *Super Voice Girls*, it attracted an astounding 400 million viewers in March 2006 when a lanky teen from Mongolia known as "the sour yogurt girl" competed for the top honor. Shanghai Media, which produces the show, is also pioneering Internet protocol television, charging $7.50 per month.

Like everywhere else, though more so, Internet usage has exploded in China, with more than double the number of netizens (150 million in 2006) than members of the Communist Party, making Baidou, China's version of Google, one of the world's top companies. There are 75 million blogs in China today, and counting.

But, as Google and Yahoo have found out there is a distinct cast of "Asian values" to the whole media scene in China with which the free-wheeling Western web clashes. Every Chinese university has its own cadre of "moderators" who try to guide chat rooms and discussions, including erasing entire entries when they feel they are not appropriate according to "The Eight Honors and Disgraces" code of "socialist morality."[16] These are: Love the country; do it no harm; – Serve the people; do no disservice. – Follow science; discard ignorance. – Be diligent; not indolent. – Be united; help each other; make no gains at other's expense. – Be honest and trustworthy; do not spend ethics for profits. – Be disciplined and law-abiding; not chaotic and lawless. – Live plainly, struggle hard; do not wallow in luxuries and pleasures.[17]

Ultimately, of course, it is not possible to effectively crack down on mass-self communication without reading every single message that passes through cyberspace. As many Chinese students know well, it doesn't take a rocket scientist to not use the "search words" employed by the virtual sensors.

No doubt, the form of modernization that will emerge will be somewhere between the wild openness of the West and the most ardent efforts of Confucian elders. "It is not possible anymore to effectively censor the flow of information," says Singapore's foreign minister George Yeo. "But if you make a big fuss over an issue you cause a dialogue in society over what is good or bad. The point of censorship is symbolic. It establishes a difference between right and wrong. It is what keeps society together and aware of what it stands for."

Clearly one of the main concerns of China's authorities is not only holding on to its non-Western culture, but also to its cultural and information market place. This was made clear enough in the fall of 2006 when Xinhua Press Agency mandated that Bloomberg, AP, and other press agencies could only be distributed in the country through Xinhua itself.

Market-Leninist censorship is most obvious in the movie industry, where, as noted earlier, China severely limits the total number of international films to 20 per year – from Europe, America, and other Asian countries – which usually means no more than two or three US films appear in any given year. China also freely excises anything in any film that might reflect badly on China's image, whether a sex scene in Ang Lee's *Lust-Caution* or a dank and garbage-strewn alley in Shanghai shown in *Mission Impossible III*.

Ha Jin, the Chinese writer in exile who won the National Book Award for *Waiting* in 2003 explains why, for this reason, he writes in English instead of Chinese:

> The Chinese Government and the authorities try to manipulate culture for their own ends. If I wrote in Chinese, I couldn't avoid that. When a movie is made, officials have a meeting where they all give their two cents about how it should end.

> This has even happened to Zhang Yimou, a great director. It creates all kinds of obstacles, even damage, to a work. If I wrote in Chinese, I'd have these kinds of endless heartaches. At least in English, my art stays intact.[18]

Chinese filmmakers and critics were embarrassed in the summer of 2008 when a Dreamworks animated film, *Kung-Fu Panda* about a Zen-like panda, became so widely popular among Chinese audiences that some nationalist voices demanded a boycott of this American film. Many wondered why such a popular film based on their own traditional tales couldn't be made in their own country. One blogger on the subject said: "China has first-class directors, first-class playwrights, first-class actors, but it's a shame that we have censorship. If they don't like your work, then there is no way [it will make it to the screen]."[19] Lu Chuan, a young film director, wrote in the *China Daily* about his efforts to make an animated movie for the Olympic Games. "I kept on receiving directions and orders from related parties on what the movies should be like. We were given very specific rules on how to promote it. Under such pressure, my co-workers and I felt stifled. The planned animation was never produced."[20]

The so-called Fifth Generation of Chinese filmmakers – named so because they are from the 1982 graduating class of the Beijing Film Academy and shared their youth in the Cultural Revolution – are familiar with this syndrome. As the *Financial Times* commented films such as *Red Sorghum* by Zhang Yimou, *Farewell My Concubine* by Chen Kaige and *The Horse Thief* by Tian Zhuangzhuang all received great acclaim, even some awards abroad, only to be kept from the screen in China and labeled as "insults" to China.[21]

However, the situation may be improving, as illustrated by Jia Zhang-ke's *Still Life*. This film, a drama about lives disrupted by the building of the Three Gorges Dam, was allowed to be shown on the big screen in Beijing in 2008, albeit, according to arts journalist Aventurina King, at 9 a.m. in the morning before an almost empty theater. "The most important thing about *Still Life*," said Jia Zhang-ke, "is that it has started to raise discussion about the kind of things cinema should deal with. People have been brought up in China to see cinema only as recreation and propaganda. Now they say, 'this film is telling us something about our lives today. Our memories. Our communities. Shouldn't this be cinema's proper role?'"[22]

Jia is hopeful: "The overall openness and freedom of China today has made it impossible for the government to restrict the filmmaking activity of a single individual," he told Phil Tinari of *Good* magazine in 2008.[23] "Working under a ban is truly nothing special; it requires no particular daring, and risks no real danger. Before, you needed access to film stock and then you had to smuggle it out of the country to edit. Now I can tuck a DV tape into my pocket. More interestingly," Zhang-ke continued, "pirated DVD versions of my films started to circulate inside China. Of course, pirating means I suffer, because we filmmakers get no revenue from distribution inside China, but ultimately, digital technology and the growth of the Internet have permanently curtailed the government's control over both filmmakers' ideology and over the apparatus of production and distribution."

For Jia, pirating is also a blessing because there is a kind of open underground of global cinema as well. "Although everyone understands that it is a crime, piracy also has opened up film to the people. Overnight, it was as if a thousand film archives opened on the street corners: art films, comedy, porn – everything is there."

As pirating evolves into legal sales and Chinese cinema finds its popular audience it may in any case bend to the market and give its Leninist censors less to worry about.

"On the one hand, *Red Sorghum* shocked world cinema and China," the actor-filmmaker Jiang Wen said in 2007 at the Venice Film Festival. "On the other hand it hasn't brought lasting change. Before *Red Sorghum* popular movie theaters were full of martial arts films. After it, they are still full of martial arts films. And *Red Sorghum*'s director is now making these films himself! So, I am not sure what has changed."[24]

Aventurina King notes the same phenomenon in pop fiction writers like the 24-year-old "post-'80s," Dolce and Gabbana-clad writer Guo Jingming. His best-selling novels like *City of Fantasy* accommodate the commercialism and non-political individualism of soft-totalitarianism which avoids social issues.[25]

Whatever the limits of cultural freedom, Chinese authorities and artists have long been rankled by the "cultural hegemony" of America. They all want China to have more influence in the world, to be respected and heard as a key player. To this end, even dissidents like the Tiananmen student leader Wang Dan were immensely proud of China hosting the Olympics. The deep reservoir of nationalism among China's current young generation erupted in the wake of global criticism over Tibet in the run up to the Olympics. Without doubt, that nationalism will find expression in cultural self-assertion against the Western narrative. As much admiration as there may be for American universities and technologies, it doesn't compare with Chinese pride over the resurrection of their civilization at a key center of gravity in the 21st century.

India, too, desires greater recognition and respect for its ancient culture in today's world. This was particularly true during the reign of the Hindu nationalist party, the BJP, whose influence remains widespread. The most vivid illustration of India's efforts to use soft power as a tool of foreign policy, Jehaghir Pocha reports, was seen when the Taliban fell in Afghanistan. Indian foreign minister Jaswant Singh, who was eager to replace Pakistan as the neighbor of influence, flew into Afghanistan as one of the first dignitaries welcoming the Karzai government bearing "not supplies of food, medicine or arms, but with tapes of Bollywood movies and music that were quickly distributed across Kabul."[26]

India's militant post-colonial political non-alignment and economic protection, combined with its huge population, fueled the growth of the world's largest filmmaking industry, Bollywood.

"Bollywood is Indian culture's secret weapon," writes Shashi Tharoor, the Indian author. "It produces five times as many films as Hollywood, taking India to the world by bringing its brand of glitzy entertainment not just to the Indian diaspora in the US and the UK but to the screens of Syrians and Senegalese." Tharoor, who was also a top aide to Kofi Annan at the UN, recalls an Indian diplomat in Damascus noting a few years ago that the only publicly-displayed portraits were those of then-President Hafez al-Assad and Amitabh Bachchan, who Tharoor describes as "India's Marlon Brando."[27]

Kishore Mahbubani, the Singaporean diplomat, sees great significance in the fact that Indian films, made for a Hindu population, appeal broadly to Muslims. "There is something unique about Indian political and social culture; a spirit of inclusiveness and tolerance pervades the Indian spirit. While the West often tries to discuss the world in black and white terms, distinguishing itself from either the evil empire or the axis of evil, the Indian mind is able to see the world in many different colors."[28]

Some hard-line Muslim conservatives, however, have reacted the same way to Indian films as to American mass culture, though, paradoxically, Hindu nationalists, in a kind of reverse fundamentalism, view Islam as a contamination of the Indian spirit because of its insistent monotheism.

In early January 2008, Afghanistan's Islamic Council met with Afghan President Hamid Karzai to complain about Christian "missionary and atheist" groups proselytizing in the country. Conversion is considered "apostasy" by these tribal leaders. But they also urged Karzai to stop local television stations from showing Indian soap operas and movies – enormously popular in Afghanistan – because they included "obscenities and scenes that were immoral."[29]

All the same, up and coming filmmakers from the Arab world seem to agree with Mahbubani's critique of Hollywood's Technicolor Manichaeism. "For the Americans, there could be no way to make films about Arab people except terrorism or fighting or war," said director Nabil Ayouch, a 38-year-old Moroccan who was inspired to make *Whatever Lola Wants* by his wife's passion for belly dancing and his own frustration with Hollywood's violence-laden depictions of cross-cultural encounters. "But there can also be some normal stories to tell, with simple people from different parts of the world meeting each other, and they don't have to be in the army, CIA or terrorists."[30]

In the huge Muslim world which once had little alternative to Western mass culture, indigenous cable channels, television and online networks have exploded. Al-Jazeera is the most famous alternative to Western news sources, but there are Al-Arabiya and others as well.

One phenomenon worth note is the fastest-selling comic book in the Arab world, *The 99*. According to *Front Line*, this comic features characters with superpowers based on the concept of Allah's 99 attributes, including wisdom and generosity, as taught in the Koran. Its creator, Naif al-Mutawa, is a 36-year-old from Kuwait who was educated in the United States and who, as a boy, devoured Marvel comics and the *Hardy Boys* mysteries. A new theme park based on this comic's heroes is in the works.

Cairo was once the center of Arab movies with directors like Youssef Chahine, whose films like *The Nile's Son* won awards at the Venice Film Festival as far back as the 1950s. Chahine, who died in 2008, both railed against rising Islamic fundamentalism and what he considered American imperialism. Now, a fledgling Arab film industry has also begun to emerge elsewhere, including in Saudi Arabia, financed by the Saudi prince Walid bin Talal, whose positive portrayal of women in oppressive Muslim societies can have revolutionary consequences. One film he produced in 2006, for example, entitled *Keif al Hal*, is about a young woman dreaming of a career instead of a husband, and the opposition to her choices by her fundamentalist brother.

Increasingly, the Arab world is turning to its own productions as a way to reinforce its identity against the West. For example, there is a new hit show on Abu Dhabi TV called *Million's Poet* modeled on *American Idol*. Success encouraged a second show *The Prince of Poets*. "We grow very fast but we need to protect our culture," says Mohammed Khalaf el Mazrouei, director general of the Abu Dhabi Authority for Culture and Heritage. "We brought poetry back to life and gave it prestige."[31]

In Cairo, Ahmed Abu Haiba, an Egyptian playwright and TV producer, has created a more chaste Arabic version of *Friends* called *Boys and Girls* and an Oprah-style show featuring a mullah as the host. "I want a new Islamic media," Abu Haiba says. "My point is not to condemn the West, but to build my own culture with its own seeds. I am more worried about Western culture than politics. It affects our thinking and ideals. It's a major danger we're facing in our beliefs, role models, and habits. If I lose my culture I become a stranger in my own country."[32] Speaking of the kind of phenomenon Abu Haiba represents, Emile Slailaty, a video director in Beirut, says of the new Arab search for identity in the media: "They want to be free and Westernized, but at the same time they want to be conservative."[33]

Efforts that don't get the balance right in the Muslim world have been met with considerable controversy.

In Afghanistan, a new show was launched in 2007 entitled *Afghan Star*, modeled after *American Idol* where contestants vie for the prize of $5,000. Though filled with patriotic songs about national unity and ordinary love songs with tame lyrics like "Oh my dear, when are you going to be my guest?" the show has outraged conservative mullahs. Seeing the performance of women as immoral, they want the show banned by the Ministry of Culture.[34]

With the explosion of satellite channels across the Arab world, music video clips in the mode of MTV have become widespread, creating new stars and avid legions of fans. They have also met with resistance. In April 2008, all but one of the members of Bahrain's Islamist-dominated parliament approved a motion urging the government to ban a planned performance by the Lebanese singer Haifa Wehbe. They felt the pop star's performance would be sexually provocative, "violating Islamic conventions and Bahrain's traditions."[35]

This controversy in the small island nation, which is one of America's closest geopolitical allies in the region, followed on a similar contretemps earlier in the year when a public outcry forced the Arabic version of *Big Brother*, renamed *Al-Ra'is* (The Boss), to suspend filming. Several Bahrainian women's groups had protested the show outside the Information Ministry building. One 34-year-old school teacher, Shahnaz Rabi'i, told the BBC: "I have watched this show and it must be stopped. Our religion has strong values which say boys and girls should not mix together. This program is a threat to Islam. This is entertainment for animals."[36]

In Cairo, video clips by the pop singer Ruby, popular among the young and affluent, have caused a reaction among others in Egypt, which has grown increasingly Islamist and socially conservative since the liberal 1970s. Because of her vamping, raunchy style and revealing clothing some conservative members of parliament have even called for a ban on her videos. Mohammed Ajami, 30, who is an assistant university lecturer, told the BBC in 2005 that Ruby's style has spread "like wildfire" among his students:

> They memorize her lyrics by heart, and they forget about anything else. Their culture is a mixture of bad influences that lead them away from Islam. They have no dreams except feeding their instincts and living like their fellows in the West. They gain the bad things from Western culture – like free relationships between men and women.[37]

*Noor*, the Turkish soap opera in which a handsome husband is supportive of his wife's ambitions outside the home, has stirred considerable controversy and riled clerics in Saudi Arabia, where it is watched by 3 to 4 million viewers daily, for being "un-Islamic."

It goes without saying that the broader development of indigenous media around the globe will be idiosyncratic according to the ebb and flow of the times and the balance of power within a given cultural setting. In some places, cinema, TV, and video entertainment will end up mimicking the worst of American mass culture, creating a backlash. Others will seek a balance. Still others, like the Turkish film *Valley of the Wolves*, mentioned earlier in the book, will be anti-Semitic, nationalistic, and anti-American.

Hopefully, the growing global sensibility in all national cultures, including in America, will demonstrate some propriety in terms of the moral norms of others as well as mitigate populist marketing ploys to sell images at home at the expense of the unfamiliar world beyond one's own borders.

The most exciting possibility is that Hollywood itself will take on a more cosmopolitan cast. Because of the historically cumulative effect of Hollywood's concentration of talent and technology, it may not to be displaced so much as evolve into a factory of global dreams – a new global cinema – that tells the stories of the whole world. In a sense, Hollywood could well return full circle to its origins as the production site for the hopes and dreams of a cosmopolitan, immigrant culture. But instead of Billy Wilder, Fred Zinneman, or other European directors dominating the scene, we will find Ang Lee, Zhang Yimou, Alfonso Cuarón, Alejandro González Iñárritu, Pedro Almodóvar, Guillermo del Toro, and others.

This possible future was most palpably felt in the 2007 Hollywood awards season. Films by foreigners such as *Babel*, that made little at the box office, won the top awards, while the big Hollywood blockbusters, which make all the money, much of it abroad, were virtually ignored. Even Clint Eastwood's acclaim that time around was due to his portrayal of the Iwo Jima battle from a foreign (Japanese) angle. Though in the end Martin Scorsese's *The Departed* won the Oscars that year, it was more a slap on the back to one of the industry's own than an indicator of the deeper trend.

Alejandro González Iñárritu's *Babel* explored how the fates of the far flung from Mexico to Morocco to Japan are linked in unsuspecting ways by the threads of globalization. Pedro Almodóvar's *Volver*, a Spanish film for which Penélope Cruz had an Oscar nomination for best actress, is a convoluted tale of women coping with generations of abuse from husbands and fathers who find within themselves the resources to act and survive on their own.

These films were critically acclaimed because they managed to break the cycle of remakes in which Hollywood has been stuck by telling new stories – something American filmmakers, who have prided themselves on their imagination and originality, once excelled at.

These days, with ever fewer exceptions, American filmmakers too often grind out formulaic shock-and-awe blockbusters with the proverbial gratuitous violence, sex, and special effects that may be winning the battle of Monday-morning grosses, but are losing the war for hearts and minds. For all their brawn, American filmmakers, like the generals in Iraq, are in danger of losing the battle of stories that matter.

As we have argued, now that globalization has moved us all into the same neighborhood, more and more people out there on the former cinematic periphery want to see their own stories on the screen, to see what is in their imagination and culture, at least as much as they might enjoy the latest offerings from LucasFilm or Pixar. This has led to more cultural competition, and even collaboration within the Hollywood template.

It is *Babel*'s González Iñárritu who has best captured what's happening. "The world is changing," he says. "The film community is now a global film community. It's not anymore about cultural barriers or language barriers. Its emotion and humanity. We are using the power of cinema to cross borders. We understand that now there's a connection that needs to happen. Everyone has talked about economic globalization, but globalization hasn't been integrated into the cultural mindset. Film can help connect those dots." In our global age movies must expose "the point of view of others, of those on the other side," he says.[38]

If González Iñárritu is right, this development perhaps presages the arrival of a new era of "blended" or "hybrid" popular culture in which the Hollywood infrastructure and well-honed production values will become less an American industry than a global one where stories that matter to our lives by connecting to our experience are on display as much as gore and surround sound.

Of course, there will always be a role for shock-and-awe blockbusters just as there will be for aircraft carriers, and audiences will flock to such spectacular diversions. But the hope held out by trailblazers like González Iñárritu is that Hollywood can be an instrument of real communication across cultures in an information age where precious little knowledge of others is sprinkled among the pixels.

González Iñárritu's new sensibility is only one aspect of the globalization of Hollywood. More concerned with market share than cultural cross-pollination, Disney among other companies is seeking to re-brand itself as global instead of the iconic American brand it once was by setting up studios for joint production of local stories in China and India, some of which will flow back into the American market. One early case in point is the Disney production of the Chinese fable, *Mulan*, which was a hit with children in the US. Sony, Warner Brothers, and Viacom are also seeking out joint-production deals in Asia.

When Bob Iger arrived at the head of Disney after Michael Eisner was booted by the board in 2005, he immediately focused on "localization" as the best way into the huge growth potential of the international market. A localization strategy allows a company like Disney to get around the limits like the 20 foreign films a year allowed in by the Chinese film board. Media companies can only salivate at the fact that there are only 3,600 screens in China compared to 30,000 in the US, making China, in film parlance, "grossly under-screened."[39]

"We want to be regarded as the Chinese Walt Disney Co. We don't want to be regarded just as the Walt Disney Co. operating in China," Stanley Cheung, executive vice-president and managing director of Disney Co. Great China, told *Variety* in

June 2007. "To do that we have to go beyond lifting the stuff we've done internationally and putting it in China."[40]

After distributing films such as *The Lion King* and TV shows such as *Lost* and *Desperate Housewives* in China since 1995, Disney made a big leap in 2007 by releasing a Chinese-made feature, *The Magic Gourd*, which made $2.1 million within the first two weeks of its release on 300 screens.[41] *The Magic Gourd* is a "family values" tale about a boy whose wishes are granted by a magic gourd only at the expense of others. The film was shot in Mandarin with a Cantonese dubbed version. The theme song was sung by a *Super Girl* contest winner – a Chinese version of *American Idol* – named Zhang who was the poster girl for the show's sponsor, Mengniu Dairy, now also a Disney partner in China.[42] As part of its Pan-Asian strategy, Disney has distribution rights for *The Magic Gourd* in Taiwan, Singapore, Malaysia, the Philippines, and Thailand.

On Memorial Day 2007, Disney released *Pirates of the Caribbean: At World's End*, to 10,000 theaters in 104 countries. The film was cast with a global audience in mind, including Asian star Chow Yun-Fat. "It's truly what I'd call the modern-day Disney franchise," Mark Zoradi, president of Walt Disney Studio's marketing and distribution department told the *New York Times*. "We had such an international cast, we had a story that wasn't landlocked to North America so this was the absolute perfect movie to open on a global basis. That was the strategy."[43]

In India, Disney already has an up-and-running Disney Channel, operates Toon Disney and the Hungama on-line and produces local TV shows such as *Vicky aur Vetal* and *Dhoom Machao Dhoom*. In 2007, Disney entered into a joint venture with Yash Raj Films to co-produce one animated movie a year.[44] In April 2008, Warner Brothers signed a multi-picture deal with India's Ocher Studios to make regional-language pictures which Warner's will release. It is also making its first animation feature in India with Goel Screencraft.[45]

In one sense, these co-production deals between American and foreign companies are nothing new. As the film historian Vanessa Schwartz reminds us in her study of the early years of the Cannes Film Festival, a kind of sub-globalization of culture also took place from the immediate post-WWII era through the '60s when films like *An American in Paris*, *Gigi*, and *Funny Face* were all joint American–European productions even before the French new wave and the Italian realist films coursed back through the Hollywood distribution networks to the US.

In the 1960s, United Artists had a very active role in Europe. It financed the Clint Eastwood westerns made in Spain and some of the Fellini movies. They were made specifically for the world market, excluding the United States. The fact that they caught fire after the fact was a surprise. The original Bernardo Bertolucci movie, *Last Tango in Paris* with Marlon Brando, was financed with Europeans in mind because the feeling was that it would do very well in Europe. The fact that it got a great review by Pauline Kael and launched the movie in the United States with an "X" rating surprised everyone at United Artists.

Indeed, as Schwartz argues, it was in those years when Cannes became not just a film festival, but also a festival of images thanks to the explosive arrival of the paparazzi which made stars into international celebrities. But, as with the birth of Hollywood, this was really a broader Westernization of culture than the globalization we see today, which includes Asia, Latin America, and elsewhere.[46]

Schwartz is quite right on the larger point, as we have argued throughout this book, that images are agents of the globalization of culture.

In the global media landscape of tomorrow where the stories of others on the rise compete with our own, where does the unique sensibility of American culture fit in? What can it offer? In what way can that sensibility, expressed through the various platforms of the evolving media, help restore America's own image?

## Notes

1. Ma, Y.-Y. "Paths of Globalization: From the Berbers to Bach." *International Herald Tribune.* January 29, 2008 (from Global Viewpoint).
2. Pocha, J. "The Rising 'Soft Power' of India and China." *New Perspectives Quarterly* (Winter 2003), vol. 20, no. 1, pp. 4–13.
3. Brennan, S. "Simpsons' News Piques Interest of Foreign Press." *The Hollywood Reporter,* September 18, 2008.
4. Chaffin, J. "Hispanics Warm to Telenovelas with an American Twist." *Financial Times,* May 25, 2006.
5. Hawley, C. "World Staying Tuned to Mexico's Telenovelas." *Arizona Republic,* September 23, 2004.
6. Hawley, C. "World Staying Tuned to Mexico Telenovelas." *Arizona Republic,* September 23, 2004.
7. Lizarzaburu, J. "How Telenovelas Conquered the World." *BBC News,* April 1, 2006.
8. Fernandez, M. E. "Television's Foreign Affair." *Los Angeles Times,* April 20, 2008.
9. Fernandez, M. E. "Television's Foreign Affair." *Los Angeles Times,* April 20, 2008.
10. Remarks by Sumner Redstone at the Nielsen Media and Money Conference, New York, November 7, 2007.
11. Remarks by Sumner Redstone at the Nielsen Media and Money Conference, New York, November 7, 2007.
12. "From Mosque to Multimedia." Interview with Nathan Gardels, in N. Gardels (ed.) (1997) *The Changing Global Order.* Blackwell, p. 71.
13. "From Mosque to Multimedia." Interview with Nathan Gardels, in N. Gardels (ed.) (1997) *The Changing Global Order.* Blackwell, p. 71.

14. Yew, L. K. "China Must Convince the World Its Rise is Peaceful." *New Perspectives Quarterly* (Spring 2008), vol. 25, no. 2, p. 23.
15. Mahbubani, K. (2008) *The New Asian Hemisphere: The Irresistible Shift of Global Power to the East.* PublicAffairs, p. 148.
16. French, H. W. (2006) "As Chinese Students Go Online, Little Sister Is Watching." *New York Times,* May 9, 2006.
17. Dan, L. (2006) New Moral Yardstick: "8 Honors, 8 Disgraces." Chinese Government's Official Web Portal. April 5.
18. Mahbubani, K. (2008) *The New Asian Hemisphere: The Irresistible Shift of Global Power to the East.* PublicAffairs, p. 148.
19. Pocha, J. "Individualism Arrives in China." An Interview with Ha Jin. *New Perspectives Quarterly* (Winter 2003), vol. 20, no. 1, pp. 13–21.
20. Chuan, L. "Kung Fu Panda Gives Food for Thought." *China Daily,* May 7, 2007 (distributed by Xinhua).
21. Andrews, N. "The China Syndrome." *Financial Times,* December 14, 2007.
22. Andrews, N. "The China Syndrome." *Financial Times,* December 14, 2007.
23. Jia Zhang-ke "Moving Pictures." *GOOD Magazine,* May–June 2008, p. 72.
24. Andrews, N. "The China Syndrome." *Financial Times,* December 14, 2007.
25. King, A. "China's Pop Fiction." *New York Times Book Review,* May 5, 2008, p. 27.
26. Pocha, J. "The Rising Soft Power of India and China." *New Perspectives Quarterly* (Winter 2003), vol. 20, no. 1, pp. 5–9.
27. Mahbubani, K. (2008) *The New Asian Hemisphere: The Irresistible Shift of Global Power to the East.* PublicAffairs, p. 170.
28. Mahbubani, K. (2008) *The New Asian Hemisphere: The Irresistible Shift of Global Power to the East.* PublicAffairs, p. 173.
29. "Afghan Clerics Warn Karzai Against Missionaries." *New York Times,* January 6, 2008, p. 9.
30. Daragahi, B. "Some Normal Stories to Tell," *Los Angles Times,* December 10, 2007, E10.
31. Khalaf, R. "TV Poetry is Epic Success as Arabs Return to Roots." *Financial Times,* March 4, 2008, p. 8.
32. Fleishman, J. "Islam in a New World." *Los Angeles Times,* April 6, 2008.

33. Fleishman, J. "Fighting Fire With Fire." *Los Angeles Times,* April 6, 2008.
34. Boone, J. "Afghan TV Show's Search for Star Pitches Pop Culture Against Religion." *Financial Times,* March 22, 2008.
35. Harrison, F. "Lebanese Singer Causes Gulf Storm." *BBC News,* April 30, 2008.
36. "Arab Big Brother Show Suspended." *BBC News,* March 1, 2003.
37. Sharp, H. "Sexy Stars Push Limits in Egypt." *BBC News,* August 4, 2005.
38. "Hollywood Must Portray Point of View of Others." Interview with Nathan Gardels. *New Perspectives Quarterly* (Spring 2007), vol. 24, no. 2, pp. 7–9.
39. Lee, D. (2008) Memo to Mike Medavoy, "Fact and Figures for Chinese Film Industry."
40. Frater, P. "Disney Takes Local Route in China." *Variety,* June 29, 2007.
41. http://ent.sina.com.cn/m/c/2007-07013/19391636694.shtml.
42. Frater, P. "Disney Takes Local Route in China." *Variety,* June 29, 2007.
43. Zoradi, M. "Pirate's Haul So Far Estimated at $401 Million." *New York Times,* May 28, 2008.
44. Frater, P. "Disney Takes Local Route in China." *Variety,* June 29, 2007.
45. Frater, P. "WB's Indian Invasion." *Variety,* June 2, 2008.
46. Schwarz, V. (2008) *It's So French: The Cannes Film Festival and the Birth of Cosmopolitan Culture.* University of Chicago Press.

# Chapter 10

# Reinventing Cultural Diplomacy

In an open-source world, in a global glasshouse, propaganda is becoming obsolete because it can no longer trump reality. A simple Google search can unravel lies and embellishments; a cell-phone video posted on the Internet undermines anybody's attempt to airbrush history. Those beaten Tibetan monks who disappeared on Chinese TV, as we noted at the outset, popped up on YouTube. Double standards, easily revealed in our age, mark the distance between self-interest and universal principle. And everyone knows it.

In this information-flush environment, the allegiance of hearts and minds must be granted consensually by persuasion – as the result of the power of example instead of the example of power, as Bill Clinton has put it so well. Unilateral will-to-power policies backfire because they lack legitimacy. No amount of spin can turn people around when the Al Jazeeras or Al Arabiyas of the world, not to speak of CNN or the Western media or milbloggers (military bloggers), are on the case. The key, therefore, to recovering American prestige is to lead by seeking consensus for our vision of the world order, by working with others and by attracting support through sticking to our ideals in practice.

It would be a mistake to believe that when the debacle of the Iraq War and the ruinous policies of the Bush administration are behind us, all will be well once again just as after the Vietnam War, that our prestige will automatically return. It is certainly true that market democracies, most particularly the US with its flexible culture, are self-correcting because of the robust feedback open societies afford. We learn, we change. But self-correction does not mean a return to the status quo ante but to forward evolution based on new conditions.

In the Vietnam years, the world remained frozen within the Cold War framework both geopolitically and geoculturally. The Cold War prevented the freer flow of capital, skills, information, and technology across borders from taking place. This has not been true in the years since 9/11/01. In our age of future shock and accelerated change on a global scale, a torrent of transformation has flowed under the bridge from the continuing rapid growth of China to the digital democratization of information.

The changes in this period didn't start from scratch but had a running start. During the previous eight years of the Clinton presidency, it was American-led globalization that helped unleash the torrent. Paradoxically, that globalization has both bound America through deeper interdependence (for example through the current account imbalance with China that finances our consumption) and constrained its power through fostering a devolution of power to other centers, including not only the European Union but "emerging market" countries like Brazil, India, and China which have become established players.

The multipolar world order now emerging – both culturally and geopolitically – was already in the birth canal. Paradoxically, it was the reaction incited by the muscular unilateralism of the Bush administration that finally pushed it out of its post-Cold War womb. In this sense, America's waning soft power has been the midwife of the new cultural self-assertion around the world.

Finally, and perhaps most fundamentally, the years after 9/11 have led to a jaded view in world public opinion of America's universalist claims. It turns out that even this historically exceptional nation, guarantor without peer of the liberal world order, retreated like any other country from its principles when fear narrowed its perception of national interest. America is no longer the same in the eyes of the world.

The path to the recovery of American prestige offered by the traditional foreign policy establishment has been called "smart power" by Harvard professor Joe Nye. Essentially this means rebalancing hard power with a surge of soft power through enhanced educational exchanges, reinvigorated alliances and multilateral institutions, policies aimed at preserving an open world economy – "a commitment to universal rules of openness that spread the gains widely" in the words of John Ikenberry[1] – and joining the fight against poverty and global warming. In the campaign against terrorism and nuclear non-proliferation, hard power must be deployed judiciously, wrapped in the legitimacy of multilateralism but for the most exceptional cases. Smart power seeks a retreat from ideology to the pragmatism for which American leadership was once admired.

Surely, Barack Obama's proposal for "America Houses" overseas that would incorporate youth centers and libraries, particularly in the Muslim world, would be helpful, as would John McCain's idea, floated during the presidential campaign, of establishing a single, independent agency responsible for all of America's public diplomacy that would include American libraries with Internet access along with a "professional corps of public diplomacy experts who speak the local language and whose careers are spent promoting American values, ideas, culture and education."[2]

The sense behind these ideas was incorporated into legislation introduced by US Senator Sam Brownback in late 2008. His bill would establish a National Center for Strategic Communication as a stand alone agency, much like the USIA once was, to fight the "broad ideological battle" against the ideas of radical Islam. What all these proposals have in common is that they are geared to America better telling its story to the world.

But if there is any singularly poignant lesson from the disastrous course America took after 9/11 it is that any new alternative like "smart power" must be sustained by informed public support at home. Every shortcoming, misadventure, misstep, or outright catastrophe of American foreign policy can be traced to the lack of knowledge and insularity of the democratic public of the world's superpower. The information gap in our time is every bit as much a threat to national security as was any military gap during the Cold War.

In our best times, as under Franklin D. Roosevelt, including through his fire-side chats and movie trailers, American leadership understood its pedagogical function in a democracy – to argue for the best course and bring the people along by making sure they thoroughly grasp the stakes.

Never has that been more necessary than in the age of globalization where we have become inextricably linked with others of whom we often have little understanding. As we move into the future, Americans not only need to develop a cosmopolitan capacity for empathy and understanding of those with whom we share this shrinking planet; they need to be educated to embrace the rules of engagement for globalization which require forging common and fair rules of the game.

Because of our still considerable power and unique status, American leadership remains indispensable in this task of making the world safe for interdependence – a task that is in our vital long-term interest because we will not always be the top dog as power shifts in the twenty-first century. Isolationist, protectionist, nativist, nationalistic, or hubristic sentiments threaten that notion of security.

Similarly, as religious extremism, tribal intolerance, populist authoritarianism, or statist repression abroad assert themselves against the "contamination" of greater global integration, the projection of the American experience as an open, culturally plural society that works has never been more critical. That is our competitive advantage, as conveyed, with all the attendant frictions, in such films as *Crash*.

It is in this realm of shaping public opinion and awareness in support of smart power and a cosmopolitan, open culture globally that public diplomacy and Hollywood come in. They are part of the "deep coalition" required to build the cultural infrastructure of interdependence. As we have suggested throughout this book, since the reach of American mass culture and its powerful story-telling impact play such a large role in forming mindsets both at home and abroad, they must be as much a part of this effort as State Department publicists and political leadership.

As Harvard's Joe Nye has pointed out, culture is not in and of itself "soft power," but a resource that can have negative or positive influence depending on the context. How, then, can Hollywood deploy its considerable talents to produce the kind of "soft power" that can help America's story win again?

To start with, Hollywood – meaning professionally produced content for mass or niche consumption across all media platforms – should return to the ethics of one of its founders, Harry Warner. Warner believed that movies should educate as well as entertain. Understanding the power of images, he felt a responsibility not only to amuse but also to enlighten the public about the rising threat to liberal civilization posed in his day by fascism. "The motion picture producer shares this obligation with the schools, the churches, the service organizations of all kinds, which stand for tolerance, for decent thinking and fair relations with the rest of mankind," Warner wrote in 1939. "I do not mean that we should attempt, in the theater, to teach all the lessons, preach all the sermons or solve all the problems of the world. We cannot do this, but we can and should give a helping hand. The motion picture can be a great power for peace and good will or, if we shirk our obvious duty, it can stand idly by and let the world go to pot."[3]

In our day, the challenges, of course, are different, more diffuse, and more complicated – and the media platforms have vastly diversified from the silver screen to the cell phone. But as 9/11 made clear, the challenges are no less daunting in terms of calling forth gestures of responsibility.

There are two areas where the mass culture industry and public diplomacy could collaborate in purpose. It is not a matter of Hollywood following government policy; it is a matter of imparting a sensibility: First, in the promotion and defense of liberal civilization in a way, necessary in the age of the global glasshouse, that is humble and honest about the shortcomings of the liberal model of "the good life" with respect to its universal application. Second, the promotion within America of empathetic understanding of other civilizations and ways of life. Both of these efforts would, in turn, encourage cultural fusion globally, in cinema as well as in other arts and entertainment, fostering cosmopolitan awareness instead of conflict born of ignorance.

State Department publicists and Hollywood filmmakers alike, along with other professional producers of content, should not shrink before political correctness from the defense of liberal civilization. Just as in Warner films like *Confessions of a Nazi Spy* the threat today should be made clear. As a refuge and outpost of cosmopolitan humanity comprised of every ethnic, racial, and religious stripe, the American idea stands as much against the twenty-first-century challenges of Islamist extremism, ideological conformism, and nationalistic or tribal politics as against the fascism of the mid-twentieth century. Especially in our world of hybrid cultures and open societies, the dream of purity is the face of the enemy. As Paul Berman has pointed out in his essay "Terror and Liberalism," the yearning for purity – racial, ideological, or religious – is at the root of all fundamentalisms. It is the impetus of obscurantism, of the impulse to close off instead of open up, to exclude instead of embrace.

Ayaan Hirsi Ali, the media-savvy author of *Infidel*, believes Hollywood can have enormous power over the hearts and minds of the world in promoting an open global society if it takes on the task. For her, Hollywood filmmakers have as much power to shape the lives of individuals as politicians, if not more.

In her view, films like Alejandro González Iñárritu's *Babel* show what can be done. For Hirsi Ali, the star power of the movie – Brad Pitt and Cate Blanchett – was irrelevant. Its power lay in the depiction of the young Moroccan shepherd boys, brothers, who accidentally shot a tourist riding in a bus driving through the desolate countryside with a rifle left as a gift by a Japanese businessman who was on an exotic hunt.

First, the film showed the arbitrariness and brutality with which the Moroccan police treated its own citizens. But most of all, it showed a "ground reality" that ought to offer some insight into the radicalism and insurgency America faces around the world today. Despite the brutal interrogations by the authorities, the brothers, wrongly suspected of being some kind of terrorists, would not snitch on each other about who shot at the bus. After all, they were their only reality; they lived with each other day in and day out. The rest of the world was just a faraway abstraction. Loyal to the only reality they knew, their instinct was to flee when the police closed in. When one brother was shot and killed, the other became an eternal enemy of the Moroccan authorities.

For Hirsi Ali, the power of such a film lay not only in its subtle but meticulously honest portrayal of North African reality, but in the fact that the most impressive faces on the screen were not the big stars, but the dark visages of the poor and dispossessed of what we used to call "the Third World."

Cinema, she argues, can be an especially vital tool in changing behavior in the tribal or traditional societies across the Muslim world. The cinematic condemnation, for example, of genital mutilation in Africa or honor killings in Turkey, using actors in whose faces people find a reflection of their own lives, can, more than legislation by weak states, shame these practices out of existence. That kind of shame expressed by one's own kind, not actors from the West, is, for Hirsi Ali, the ultimate weapon in undermining the notion of male "honor" in whose name women are so widely mistreated. This, more than all the troops a long war against radical Islam can muster, would help the West win its battle of ideas.

Graham Fuller, a former vice-chairman of the CIA's National Intelligence Council and author of *The Future of Political Islam* has, in the face of endless political frustration, placed some hope in the power of cinema to break the shackles of dead-end mentalities on all sides in the Middle East. He was struck by the potential of three films that came out about the same time – Hany Abu Assad's *Paradise Now*, Steven Spielberg's *Munich*, and Stephen Gaghan's *Syriana* – to help the warring parties step out of themselves.

"Sadly, but not surprisingly," Fuller wrote in 2006, "Americans, Israelis and Palestinians have now regressed from their more universal and positive attributes to a psychological circling of the wagons, a reversion to the certitudes of super-patriotism, of my country right or wrong, in search of the elemental strengths of inflated nationalism in a time of trouble." As a result, Fuller, concluded, no one is willing to settle for anything less than "complete victory" – "a psychological mindset that could not be more damaging for any ultimate accommodation, reconciliation and resolution."

For Fuller, these three films open just that empathetic space by refraining from self-righteous certitudes about the moral stance of their own side. "The actual 'accuracy' of any one of these films," Fuller says, "will be debated by partisans for years, but that is not the issue. What matters is the vision of the three directors who attempt to rise above narrow patriotic certitudes and routine demonization of the enemy to suggest an examination of events at the human level and the reasons for why the 'other' is doing what he is doing."[4]

Even as it pursues this battle of ideas, America needs, at the same time, to be more honest on the global stage about the excesses of its anything-goes liberal cultural model and garner a bit more humility and magnanimity with respect to other definitions of the "good life." Should we really be so confident in our universalist assertion that our own practices of "freedom" are always better than the more restrained practices of other societies rooted in Confucian or Islamic or Hindu traditions in which community, filial responsibility, more spirituality, and less materialism have more sway than the desires of the individual? We can hardly arrogate to ourselves the role as "tutors of mankind in its pilgrimage to perfection," in the famous critique of Reinhold Niebuhr, when Britney Spears is the poster child for the American way of life.

Martha Bayles hits the nail right on the head. "The United States is now in the position of having to affirm the crucial importance of free speech in a world that has serious doubts about it. And the best way to do this is to show that freedom is self-correcting: that the American people possess not only liberty but also a civilization worthy of liberty."[5]

Instead of self-righteousness, the appropriate attitude, to paraphrase Winston Churchill on democracy, might be that liberal civilization is the most flawed there is, save for the others.

Hand in hand with this cultural humility must come not only increased information, but also empathetic understanding of others to whom we are tethered by globalization. "To be able to put oneself in another's shoes without prejudgment is an essential skill," Yo-Yo Ma has said.[6] "Empathy comes when you understand something deeply, and can thus make unexpected connections. These parallels bring you closer to things that would otherwise seem far away." In our world of specialization, compartmentalization, and distant stereotyping, empathy, for Yo-Yo Ma, "is the ultimate quality that acknowledges our identity as members of the human family."

Such knowledge, joined with a dose of humility, is what will prevent the promotion of liberal civilization from becoming, like the Iraq War, an ill-conceived adventure in the name of universal values. Such knowledge will enable us to forge a pragmatic modus vivendi with other civilizations, describing both the limits of our power as well as softer means of negotiating change while keeping the peace as a new hybrid global civilization emerges.

The next time around, we might, for example, be less hubristic about the "cakewalk" to Western-style democracy in a place like Iraq, where the president who plotted a pre-emptive strike was surprised by civil war because he only belatedly became aware of the historical rift between Shiite and Sunnis that has been going on for centuries. Next time around we might anticipate that occupying a place whose inhabitants remember the Mongols at the Gates of Baghdad in 1258 like it was yesterday might generate resistance. We might be more wary of the notion that toppling a brutal dictator like Saddam Hussein would somehow automatically release the American waiting to be born inside every Arab. Reflecting on the US mistakes in the Iraq War, the general who led the US Central Command in Iraq and Afghanistan from 2003–7, John Abizaid, tallied the cost of cultural insularity. He told the Pacific Council in July 2008 that "there was a universal transfer of cultural norms that took place in Washington. They thought the invasion of Iraq was the liberation of France as opposed to going into a Middle Eastern state rife with ethnic divisions. There was a huge cultural gap. So, we made some of the initial decisions in the war based on not understanding the culture."[7]

What this suggests is that the whole idea of public diplomacy must be turned on its head, inverted inward, to educate our own leaders, the public, and the storytellers of popular culture about the world beyond our borders.

The Muslim scholar Tariq Ramadan has rightly said that, for all its hype, the information age is an age of non-communication.[8] For all the big-screen movies, endless hours of television, Google searches, and iTune downloads, with the world a click away, Americans still have little knowledge of others globally. Since the end of the Cold War, even the fourth estate – the journalistic establishment – has dramatically retreated from global coverage just when it was most necessary.

"The weakness of America today," Zbigniew Brzezinski told Adam Garfinkle in the Spring 2008 issue of the *American Interest*,

> is that we're more democratic than we've ever been before, in the sense that popular pressures translate into policy pressures very quickly. And we're probably as ignorant as ever about the rest of the world, because everybody now lives in a kind of simplistic, trivialized virtual reality in which fact and

fiction, impressions and impulses, are mixed up in an incoherent fashion. The public really has no grasp of complexities, no sense of intellectual refinement in judging them, and our political leaders have become increasingly demagogic.

"The way George W. Bush campaigned for the war in Iraq," Brzezinski continued,

with reference to fictitious WMDs, and with sweeping, simplistic, black-and-white generalizations about freedom and tyranny, is a case in point. But he was responding to our increasingly imbecilized societal condition. This is very troublesome. The degeneration of the newspapers as a primary source of information, the collapse of serious television news programs and the emergence of this kind of instant communion between reality and virtual reality creates a collective state of mind that is not derived from rational analysis.

As newspapers in general retreat further from international and even national news coverage more and more people will get such news from websites. The danger, as is already apparent, is that they will find news where they look for it – not in an objective venue dedicated to the public interest but to a website that conforms to their ideological predisposition. This is the verdict from the success of cable news from Fox to MSNBC's Keith Olberman to John Stewart's *Daily Show* to blogs like the Huffington Post and the Rush Limbaugh talk-radio show.

British foreign minister David Miliband is fond of saying that the world is going through a "civilian surge" as technology empowers citizens to hold governments and other powers accountable through access to information. As we have argued in this book, this is very much true – as far as it goes. Shimon Peres has taken this a bit further and closer to the mark. "The mass media," he has said in one of his famous aphorisms, "have made dictatorship impossible, but democracy intolerable"[9] through its relentless search for market share by substituting knowledge for sensation of any kind, whether celebrity obsession or sex and violence for its own sake. Shock value has moved on from the edgy modernist experiment aimed at breaking molds to a marketing ploy. Indeed, what knowledge of the local tribes and Taliban did the ability of the Drudge Report impart to us by exposing the secret deployment of Prince Harry to Afghanistan?

Recently, the president of Yale University, Richard Levin, lamented the "insularity" of his students, many of whom go on to become ill-informed political leaders who make disastrous judgments in world affairs, like Yale graduate George W. Bush. And can anyone forget that former Arkansas governor and presidential candidate Mike Huckabee's bizarre response to Benazir Bhutto's assassination was to "look for the suspicious activities of Pakistanis in the US," linking them to illegal border crossings along with Mexicans?

What is true of Yale, is triply true of Hollywood, whose powerful images present America to the world and substantially shape the worldview of Americans. Often, the result is worse than no information; it is Ramboesque mal-information which casts the world in stereotypes or cardboard cutouts.

The former German foreign minister, Joschka Fischer, makes the penetrating observation that while foreign ministers once represented their country to the world, now they must represent the world to their country. Following this logic, the most important change required in the practice of public diplomacy is to follow Fischer's advice and invert its focus. The State Department, which has subsumed the United States Information Agency, should be given the mission not only of informing the world about America, but of informing the American public, starting with Hollywood, about the world out there. Above all, those who inform and educate, incidentally or purposefully, through the powerful image media need themselves to be informed.

Though it goes without saying, we'll say it anyway to avoid any confusion. By no means are we suggesting control or "guidance" of information by the state. The idea is simply that the diplomatic arm of the state, responsible for our connection with the outside world in a democracy, must assume greater responsibility in the interconnected global age for educating its citizens about realities beyond their borders.

By far, the most effective route into the hearts and minds of the public is not prosaic political speeches, as important as they may sometimes be, but through "imaginative knowledge" – literature or cinema – that shines some empathetic light for us on the lives and souls of others. More appropriately, this might be called cultural diplomacy.

What Salman Rushdie said of the role of post-national literature after 9/11 applies to cinema as well. "Literature," says Rushdie, "can take away that part of fear which is based on not knowing things."[10] Similarly, Azar Nafisi, author of *Reading Lolita in Tehran*, says "The news media is supposed to serve one aspect of our needs – information. The other aspect must be satisfied elsewhere through imaginative knowledge. Part of the reason people liked my book was because they could experience through reading it what a young girl experienced in a country called an Islamic Republic. And they realized that her desires and aspirations were not very different from their own."[11] The Turkish novelist and Nobel laureate, Orhan Pamuk makes a similar case for the imaginative art of the novel, which he sees as "based on the unique capacity of human beings to identify with the Other, even those with whom we may have no common interests."[12]

One example of empathetic cinema is the cartoon film *Persepolis* in which the Iranian narrator flees both from the virtue police at home and the nihilistic teenage posse of her student days in Vienna. Another might be Ye Lou's *Summer Palace*, a tale of existential despair among the scattered and purposeless Tiananmen Square generation looking for love as China modernizes. Danny Boyle's *Slumdog Millionnaire* offers deep insight into class and poverty in rising India. Alejandro González Iñárritu's *Babel* is a fine example of a film that purposely set out, as Iñárritu has described, "to tell the point of view of others." Echoing Yo-Yo Ma's argument for empathy, Iñárritu says "the most important thing for me was not to portray another culture in the light of our eyes, of our reality. That's a caricature, a very Occidental way to portray an African or a Mexican or a Japanese. I tried very hard to see what was important to them, to sacrifice and subordinate my point of view in order to see the drama of their world through their eyes."

"At the same time," the Mexican filmmaker continued, "the key was to give all the characters dignity. Two words guided the making of *Babel* for me: dignity and compassion. These things are normally forgotten in the making of a lot of films. Normally, there is not dignity because the poor and dispossessed in a place like Morocco are portrayed as mere victims or the Japanese are portrayed as cartoon figures with no humanity."[13]

Promoting imaginative knowledge with this ideal in mind ought to be lauded and consciously supported as a key pillar of public, or cultural, diplomacy turned inward.

Like Harry Warner, Hollywood's multitude of talents ought, on those occasions when the muse of art and conscience coincide, to devote their creativity to these two tasks – promoting and defending an open global society and educating the American public about that world. To the oft-repeated retort of Hollywood producers to this notion that "we are just a business here to entertain and make money," we offer this response: Is there really so little talent in Hollywood these days that no one can rise, on occasion, to the challenge of both education and entertainment?

In practical terms, what can be done? We know from the financial crash of 2008 that relying on the unattended market alone can be dearly damaging. The same is true, even more so, of culture. As we've discussed, the bubble of mass culture can distort communication among peoples, eclipsing some aspects of the life of nations while amplifying or exaggerating others into stereotypes. Indeed, ceding the communication among cultures to only what is commercially viable is deeply irresponsible in the age of globalization.

Of course, in a free society culture cannot be regulated like finance. Government cannot, nor should it, attempt to dictate cultural output. But, both government and the entertainment industry can ensure that counterweights – the kinds of checks and balances that exist wherever power resides in a liberal democratic society – are put in place.

Our proposal is twofold. First, the new administration should launch a major quasi-public institution – it could be called the Information and Cultural Exchange Forum – modeled on the Public Broadcasting System. Second, the entertainment industry itself should establish a Council on Cultural Relations specifically aimed at raising the global sensibilities of the storytellers in Hollywood.

The Information and Cultural Exchange Forum would be an autonomous agency subsidized as part of the State Department's public diplomacy efforts and granted tax-exempt status to encourage private contributions. Like PBS, it would be editorially independent (though, as PBS knows, no entity linked to government funds is ever fully free of political strings) and not subject to the diktat of whoever is in power at the moment.

Unlike the Voice of America, for example, the Forum would not be tied to any particular diplomatic agenda. Its broad mandate would be to "help make the world safe for interdependence" through promoting the exchange of information and culture between the US and the rest of the world.

The important distinction here is that the Forum would be structured as a two-way street. America would be hearing the story of others as well as telling its own story – an evolution of public diplomacy toward cultural exchange long sought by advocates such as Nicholas Cull of the Annenberg School at the University of Southern California.

The Forum's key objectives would include:

• Breaking the insularity of the American public by promoting the exposure of foreign films, art, theater, literature, and news in the US. The Forum would seek to build broader American audiences for the vast array of available foreign films as well as finance and arrange for the translation, publication, and review of foreign literature which, these days, barely has a presence in the US.

A further major role of the Forum would be to fill the gap created by the nearly wholesale retreat of mainstream American news organizations from extensive coverage of global news and cultural trends. It would seek, in other words, to "denationalize" the news Americans receive. The Forum would utilize various media platforms – especially an authoritative on-line newspaper/website with global links – to achieve these ends.

• Promoting the exposure of worthy American cultural products abroad that may not meet the market test of mass culture or, perhaps, the political test of embracing government policy, thus lacking the extensive distribution networks of commercial entertainment or official sanction.

One example of what we have in mind here was the British Council's sponsorship of performances of the Scottish play "Black Watch" in the US, even though it was highly critical of the Iraq war.

In short, the Forum would aim to fill out the profile of American life for the rest of the world beyond the familiar visage presented by the mass media.

- Promoting a vastly broadened direct exchange of students, journalists, intellectuals, and other cultural figures through conferences, travel, and reciprocal arrangements with education institutions abroad. This would include an enhanced emphasis on language training at all levels of US education.

As a complement to this government initiative, an industry-organized Council on Cultural Relations should be established on the model of the Council on Foreign Relations.

The CFR was established in 1921 as a means to keep the financial community informed, and to advise government, through its resident experts, about world trends as America emerged for the first time as a great power after World War I. In our day, cultural capital, so to speak, is similarly influential and those who produce it also need to better grasp the world in which they now must operate.

A consortium of studios, entertainment corporations, the Motion Picture Association, the Academy of Motion Picture Arts & Sciences and, perhaps, the Paley Museum should be organized to fund and govern the entity. Membership would be extended to movie, television, and web producers, actors, screenwriters, and directors. The CCR could stand alone as a self-funded non-profit 501(c)(3) institution with the same tax exemption as other educational entities or foundations.

Perhaps in cooperation with the Forum, the CCR would hold seminars and conferences on cultural and foreign affairs topics, invite world leaders to speak (as when the Pope was invited in 1987), organize informational trips and meetings abroad, and screen films, including foreign films. (Many Iranian films actually find their way to local specialty cinemas in Los Angeles, where there is a large Persian community. But, absent a concerted focus on exposure, not many who are associated with the business of Hollywood bother to go and see them.)

One example of a program might involve a TV series like *24*, which is widely viewed abroad, imparting a sense of cultural permission that torture is necessary, and works, in the extenuating circumstances of the war on terror. The role of the CCR would be to hold a conference on the subject, inviting the program's producers and writers as well as experts from the intelligence community and victims of torture to debate its value, but also to promote discussion among the Hollywood community itself about the responsibility of producing images, even if fictional, that nonetheless shape views of America abroad.

Martin Scorcese's Film Foundation and World Cinema Foundation clearly would have a role here in presenting cinema as part of a long heritage of artistic expression, global in scope, which must be viewed critically, not just passively.

Another such set of programs might follow the example of the Saban Center at the Brookings Institute which is putting together a project with the Writers Guild of America to explore ways to positively present Muslim characters in American TV shows and movies.

In addition, the CCR could even create an annual award for "best film, TV, or web series" that advances understanding of others or best promotes the American message of a plural and tolerant society that works.

These proposals are but two among many possible approaches to addressing the issues we've raised in this book. Our aim here is to simply suggest a way of thinking about the imperative of cultural diplomacy as both Washington and Hollywood go about their daily business.

This book was written to encourage dialogue between Hollywood and Washington about the power and importance of media in the conduct of global affairs in the 21st century.

For policymakers in Washington, the value of a reinvented cultural diplomacy along the lines we suggest ought to be self-evident. As readers of this book from Hollywood ponder our arguments for acting in the public interest, surely they also know the future of the American movie industry itself rests in capturing a bigger share of the global audience. It is thus in Hollywood's own interest to understand the world as it really is and convey that reality through its considerable talents to its audience – an audience which happens to also be the democratic public that ultimately steers American power toward glory or blunder.

## Notes

1. Ikenberry, J. "China and the Rest Are Only Joining the American-built Order." *New Perspectives Quarterly* (Summer 2008), vol. 25, no. 3, pp. 18–21.
2. Barnes, S. "Whose Face to the World?" *International Herald Tribune*, May 23, 2008.
3. Kaplan, M. and Blakley, J. (eds.) (2003) *Warner's War: Politics, Pop Culture & Propaganda in Wartime Hollywood.* The Norman Lear Center, University of Southern California, p. 12.
4. Fuller, G. "Will Groundbreaking Movies Move the Middle East?" *New Perspectives Quarterly* (Spring 2006), vol. 23, no. 2, pp. 31–3.
5. Bayles, M. "The Ugly Americans: How Not to Lose the Global Culture War." *AEI Online*, December 4, 2008.
6. Ma, Y.-Y. "Paths of Globalization: From the Berbers to Bach." *New Perspectives Quarterly* (Spring 2008), vol. 25, no. 2, pp. 19–21.
7. Remarks at the Pacific Council on International Policy, Los Angeles, July 21, 2008.
8. Ramadan, T. "The Global Ideology of Fear." *New Perspectives Quarterly* (Winter 2006), vol. 23, no. 1, p. 12.
9. Conversation with Nathan Gardels, Belveder Hotel, Davos, Switzerland, January 27, 1998.
10. "Literature Can Close the Fear Gap." Interview with Michael Skafidas. *New Perspectives Quarterly* (Summer 2005), vol. 22, no. 3, pp. 7–12.

11.  "Fiction: Open Space in a Closed Society." Interview with Michael Skafidas. *New Perspectives Quarterly* (Summer 2005), vol. 22, no. 3, pp. 12–15.
12.  Gardels, N. (2008) "The Art of the Novel is Anti-Political." Interview with Paul Holdengraber. *New Perspectives Quarterly* (Spring 2008), vol. 25, no. 2, p. 90.
13.  "Hollywood Must Portray Point of View of Others." Interview with Nathan Gardels. *New Perspectives Quarterly* (Spring 2007), vol. 24, no. 2, pp. 7–9.

# Six Key Concepts of This Book

*For the convenience of the reader we summarize here the key themes of this book:*

**1. Future conflicts will be about contending values in the global public square created by the media.** The conflicts of the future are going to be as much about the abundant cultural flows of the global information economy as about the scarcity of resources. This is because contending values have been crowded into a common public square created by freer trade, the spread of technology, and the planetary reach of the media.

Only in such a world could a cartoon of the Prophet Mohammed in an obscure Danish daily newspaper ignite rage across the vast and distant Islamic world. Only in such a world would bloodied Tibetan monks be censored out of Chinese TV news reports only to show up on You Tube. Only in such a world would the Vatican launch an all out assault on the *Da Vinci Code* movie to convince audiences that popular fiction is inferior to eternal truth.

In cultural matters, where there is friction there is also fusion. Clashes are part of the process of negotiation that is forging a global cosmopolitan commons.

2. **Power lies with the image.** In this global public square power lies with the image since most people apprehend reality emotionally not rationally. In forming a worldview, people tend to buy into a narrative based on what images they identify with, images that confer dignity, recognition, and status within their culture. It is why a middle-aged man buys a Porsche or why a teenager desires a pair of Pumas or whatever the latest fashion promoted by the media; its why Saddam played "My Way" at his birthday parties and why humiliated youth in Gaza identified with Al Qaeda taking down the Twin Towers on 9/11.

3. **Because of its global reach, American popular culture is as much a player in international affairs as the formal institutions of American foreign policy.** Lacking direct experience in the reality of others since less than 10 percent travel abroad every year, most Americans, who are also largely "post-textual", get their views of foreigners (other than from the land from which they immigrated) from television and movies. The opposite is also true: American movies, TV shows, and pop music provide the images of America to the rest of the world.

Because of the historically unique power of our media-industrial complex to project America's way of life to the world, America in the eyes of the world is not only about who we are and what we do, but also how we present ourselves through Hollywood films and popular culture. It is all of a piece.

4. **In the global media age America must compete for hearts and minds.** Though America's media-industrial complex, including Hollywood – the greatest projector of images in the history of human civilization – once dominated images, icons, and information globally, that is less and less true every day.

Prosperity and the spread of technology has enabled and empowered others to tell their own stories and put their own myths on the silver screen; the digital distribution revolution has democratized global information flows and diversified platforms to include not only TV and the PC, but also the cell phone screen. Increasingly, cultural flows are a two-way street. The need for America to compete for allegiance is especially true after the Iraq war, Guantanamo, Abu Ghraib, and Katrina. If politics in the information age is about whose story wins, America has been on a losing streak. America's preaching to China about human rights and the self-determination of the Tibetan people rang hollow to whole swaths of global public opinion after Abu Ghraib and the pre-emptive invasion and occupation of Iraq.

Certainly, the election of Barack Obama has restored a good deal of sheen to America's faded luster. Many who doubted that American democracy was still vital enough to deliver a black president saw their faith restored. Even so, America, like everyone else, has to compete in this space of power for hearts and minds and can no longer assume that much of the world will readily buy into its narrative.

Others are contending for their own way. The richest woman in China, who rose from humble circumstances to become a billionaire through recycling the cardboard boxes in which freer trade is packed, is every bit as compelling a story as Horatio Alger pulling himself up by his bootstraps. Qing Dynasty soaps, South Korean soaps, and Latin telenovelas now compete with *Days of Our Lives* and other popular American fare in the daily media diets of the world audience.

**5. Liberty is our message, but we are not the tutor of mankind on its pilgrimage to perfection.** The most powerful American message in modern times that is transmitted through our Hollywood films, TV shows, and popular music – the message of liberty, that "each individual can write his or her own narrative" in a meritocracy if they work hard and keep their character – is challenged by the postmodern "anything goes if it expands market share" entertainment values of bling and celebrity. This creates conflict with those who want to maintain the integrity of their own indigenous ways as well as with the essential message of mainstream religions, including Christianity, Islam, and Judaism, which emphasize less materialism and more piety. It's the Pope vs. Madonna; it's MTV vs. the headscarf.

**6. Hollywood needs to educate as well as entertain.** To compete for hearts and minds in this global media age, American popular culture needs to educate as well as entertain. When creativity and conscience coincide, Hollywood needs to reach above shock and awe blockbusters to promote liberal civilization based on our competitive advantage – a racially and culturally plural cosmopolitan society that works – against those who seek the enclosed and fearful purity of religion, tribe, or nation. To be credible in the global glasshouse created by the media, such an initiative at cultural diplomacy, however, also needs to convey humility about the limits of liberal culture and recognize that "we are not the tutor of mankind on its pilgrimage to perfection." Should we be so proud that Britney, whose meltdown was followed in every detail by the media, is the poster child of our way of life?

American entertainment and the media also need to provide empathetic insight to our own woefully insular public about others of whom we know little, but with whom we are inexorably tethered by globalization. American entertainment has a special responsibility in this task since most Americans get their images of the world through movies and TV, and most of the world gets its image of us from American movies and TV. For that reason, Hollywood is a key player in the "deep coalition" required to support a "smart power" foreign policy and build a global cultural infrastructure that will make the world safe for interdependence.

# About the Authors

Nathan Gardels has been editor of *New Perspectives Quarterly* since it began publishing in 1985. He has served as editor of *Global Viewpoint* and *Nobel Laureates Plus* (services of Los Angeles Times Syndicate/Tribune Media) since 1989. These services have a worldwide readership of 35 million in 15 languages.

Gardels has written widely for *The Wall Street Journal*, *Los Angeles Times*, *New York Times*, *Washington Post*, *Harper's*, *U.S. News & World Report*, and the *New York Review of Books*. He has also written for foreign publications, including *Corriere della Sera*, *El Pais*, *Le Figaro*, the *Straits Times* (Singapore), *Yomiuri Shimbun*, *O'Estado de Sao Paulo*, *The Guardian*, *Die Welt*, and many others. His books include, *At Century's End: Great Minds Reflect on Our Times* and *The Changing Global Order*.

Since 1986, Gardels has been a Media Leader of the World Economic Forum (Davos). He has lectured at the Islamic Educational, Scientific and Cultural Organization (ISESCO) in Rabat, Morocco and the Chinese Academy of Social Sciences in Beijing, China. Gardels was a founding member at the New Delhi meeting of Intellectuels du Monde and a visiting researcher at the USA-Canada Institute in Moscow before the end of the Cold War. He has been a member of the Council of Foreign Relations, as well as the Pacific Council, for many years, and is a Senior Fellow at the UCLA School of Public Affairs.

From 1983 to 1985, Gardels was executive director of the Institute for National Strategy where he conducted policy research at the USA-Canada Institute in Moscow, the People's Institute of Foreign Affairs in Beijing, the Swedish Institute in Stockholm, and the Friedrich Ebert Stiftung in Bonn. Prior to this, he spent four years as key advisor to the Governor of California on economic affairs, with an emphasis on public investment, trade issues, the Pacific Basin, and Mexico.

Gardels holds degrees in Theory and Comparative Politics and in Architecture and Urban Planning from UCLA. He lives in Los Angeles with his wife, Lilly, and two sons, Carlos and Alexander.

Sample some of the best American films over the past 35 years and there's a good chance **Mike Medavoy** played a role in the success of many of them. From agent to studio chief, he has been involved with over 300 feature films.

Medavoy began his career at Universal Studios in 1964. He rose from the mailroom to become a casting director. In 1965, he became an agent at General Artist Corporation and then vice-president at Creative Management Agency. Joining International Famous Agency as vice-president in charge of the motion picture department in 1971, he worked with such prestigious clients as Steven Spielberg, Francis Ford Coppola, Terrence Malick, Jane Fonda, Donald Sutherland, Gene Wilder, Jeanne Moreau, and Jean-Louis Trintignant among others. United Artists brought him in as senior vice president of production in 1974 where he was part of the team responsible for *One Flew Over the Cuckoo's Nest*, *Rocky*, and *Annie Hall,* all of which won the Best Picture Oscars over three successive years in 1975, 1976, and 1977. Other notable pictures included *Apocalypse Now*, *Raging Bull*, *Network*, and *Coming Home*.

In 1978 Medavoy co-founded Orion Pictures. During his tenure *Platoon*, *Amadeus*, *Robocop*, *Hannah and Her Sisters*, *The Terminator*, *Dances with Wolves*, and *Silence of the Lambs* were released. In 1990, after 12 fruitful years at Orion, Medavoy became chairman of TriStar Pictures. Under his aegis, critically acclaimed box office successes *Philadelphia*, *Terminator 2: Judgment Day* (with Carolco), *Sleepless in Seattle*, *Cliffhanger* (with Carolco), *The Fisher King*, *Legends of the Fall*, and Steven Spielberg's *Hook* debuted. Of all the films Medavoy has been involved with, 16 have been nominated for Best Picture Oscars and seven have won Best Picture Academy Awards and numerous international festival awards.

Medavoy has made a mark not only within his industry but in his community as well. He has received numerous awards, including the 1992 Motion Picture Pioneer of the Year Award, "Career Achievement" Awards from UCLA (1997), the University of Central Florida (2002), and the 1999 UCLA Neil H. Jacoby Award, which honors individuals who have made exceptional contributions to humanity. In 2001, he received the inaugural Fred Zinnemann Award presented by the Anti-Defamation League and in 2002 received the Israel Film Festival's Lifetime Achievement Award. In 2004, he was given the Louis B. Mayer Business Award, Leader of the Year Award from Florida Atlantic University, and the Lifetime Achievement Award at the Cannes Film Festival (1998). In 2005, Medavoy was the recipient of UCLA School of Theater, Film, and Television and Producers Guild of America Vision Award. In 2007 he received the Stella Adler Actors' Studio Marlon Brando Award. He has also served as chairman of the jury of the Tokyo Film Festival, advisor to the Shanghai Film Festival, and advisor to the St Petersburg Festival, and was a member of the board of the academy of Motion Picture Arts & Sciences (1977–1981). Medavoy is also one of the original founding members of the Board of Governors of the Sundance Institute (1978) and is chairman emeritus of the American Cinematheque and the Stella Adler Actors' Studio. In addition, Medavoy was also inducted into the Hollywood Walk of Fame and received a star on Hollywood Boulevard (2005). In July 2008 he was awarded a Lifetime Achievement Award from the Jerusalem Film Foundation. He was named Chevalier of the French Legion of Honor in 2009.

Extending his involvement in the community, Medavoy was appointed to the Board of Directors of the Museum of Science and Industry in Los Angeles by former Governor Jerry Brown and was appointed by Mayor Richard Riordan as Commissioner on the Los Angeles Board of Parks and Recreations. He is a member of the Board of Directors of the University of Tel Aviv. He also serves on the Board of Trustees of the UCLA Foundation and is a member of the Chancellor's Associates, the Dean's Advisory Board at the UCLA School of Theater, Film, and Television, and the Alumni Association's Student Relations Committee. He is also the Co-Chairman of the Burkle Center for UCLA's Center for International Relations and served as a member of the Board of Advisors at the Kennedy School at Harvard University for five years, and is a member of the Council on Foreign Relations. Medavoy is also a member of the Baryshnikov Arts Center Advisory Committee. The BAC is an international center for artistic experimentation and collaboration, providing unique opportunities for the professional development of emerging and mid-career artists from around the world and across disciplines.

In 2002, Governor Gray Davis appointed Medavoy to the California Anti-Terrorism Information Center's Executive Advisory Board.

Today, as chairman and co-founder of Phoenix Pictures, Mike Medavoy has amongst other films brought to the screen *The People vs. Larry Flynt*, *The Mirror Has Two Faces*, *U-Turn*, *Apt Pupil*, *The Thin Red Line*, *The Sixth Day*, *Basic*, and *Holes*. These films have received many nominations and won two Golden Bears at the Berlin Film Festival and five Golden Satellite Awards, a cinematography award for John Toll from the ASC, and nominations from the DGA and WGA for Terrence Malick. Two of his films, *The Thin Red Line* and *The People vs. Larry Flint*, a Milos Forman movie, received Academy nominations.

Recently Phoenix also released, among others, *All The King's Men* (starring Sean Penn, Jude Law, Kate Winslet, Anthony Hopkins, and Mark Ruffalo, written and directed by Steven Zaillian), *Zodiac* (starring Jake Gyllenhaal, Robert Downey Jr., and Mark Ruffalo, directed by David Fincher), *Miss Potter* (starring Rene Zellweger and Ewan McGregor, directed by Chris Noonan), and *Pathfinder* (starring Karl Urban, directed by Marcus Nispel), and has started production on both *Shutter Island*, a film directed by Martin Scorsese, starring Leonardo DiCaprio, and *Shanghai*, starring John Cusack, Gong Li, Ken Watanabe, and Chow Yun-Fat.

In 2002, Simon & Schuster published Medavoy's bestselling book, *You're Only As Good As Your Next One: 100 Great Films, 100 Good Films and 100 For Which I Should Be Shot*, which was subsequently released in paperback in 2003.

Throughout his career Mike Medavoy has been active in politics. In 1984, he was Co-Finance Chair of the Gary Hart campaign. He also actively participated in President Clinton's election campaigns in 1992 and 1996. In 2008, he supported the candidacy of Barack Obama, and his wife, Irena, was the co-finance chair.

Mike Medavoy was born in Shanghai, China in 1941 of Russian–Jewish parents, and lived in Chile from 1947 to 1957. He graduated with honors in history from UCLA in 1963. He is married to Irena Medavoy, a founder of Team Safe-T and a charity executive and fundraiser for the Industry Task Force. Irena is also a national finance chair for Senator Obama.

Mike Medavoy has two sons, Brian and Nicholas, and resides in Beverly Hills, California.

# Acknowledgments

Except for brief stints in Washington and London, I have been based in Los Angeles for the past 20 years as I roamed the globe and wrote about world affairs as editor-in-chief of *NPQ*, the journal of social and political thought published by Wiley-Blackwell, and Global Services of the *Los Angeles Times* Syndicate/Tribune Media.

On my travels, the powerful presence of American mass culture, even in the most remote villages in China along the interior reaches of the Yangtze River, in the jungles of Central America or the Jordanian desert, never ceased to amaze me. But what amazed me more was how the East Coast-based foreign policy establishment in the United States mostly ignored this vast influence of Hollywood and pop music in their analyses of America's role in the world. Joe Nye at Harvard was one of the very few who tried to capture it with his concept of "soft power."

Over the years, Mike Medavoy, one of the smartest, most perceptive, and most politically connected producers in Hollywood, and I would often meet to ponder this paradox. About three years ago, we met for lunch at The Grill in Beverly Hills and discussed a talk I had given on "the rise and fall of American 'Soft power'" to the Strategic Assessments

Group of the CIA and as the inaugural lecture for the Globalization Awards at the UCLA School of Public Affairs.

In that moment when American prestige had sunk so miserably, thanks to the pre-emptive war in Iraq that had gone so wrong, we decided to undertake a more systematic examination of Hollywood's influence on the hearts and minds of global public opinion and American popular imagination alike. The result is this book.

Over the years as this project evolved we consulted friends far and wide, and are thankful for their input. These include Marty Kaplan and Johanna Blakeley of the Norman Lear Center; Geoff Cowen, Manuel Castells, and Nicholas Cull of the Annenberg School of Communications at USC; Alejandro González Iñárritu, Al Carnesale, Patt Morrison, John Dean, and Mary Matalin, as well as others who were kind enough to read the draft and offer the blurbs for the back cover. We would also like to thank Victoria Oberfeld and Fernando Botero for granting rights to the cover image from Botero's stunning series of paintings on "Abu Ghraib."

We are most appreciative that Doug McKay and Racheline Benveniste of Phoenix Pictures graciously lifted their attention from plowing through scripts to help read and prepare this manuscript. Richard D. Juden also provided help throughout the project.

Above all, my thanks go especially to my wife Lilli, as well as my two sons Carlos and Alexander. Though they've heard it all before, they still listen.

Nathan Gardels

At the time of writing this book, I enter the 45th year of my being in the business. It's been – and continues to be – a constant challenge. Over the years I have taken on and continue to enjoy the whole experience. In some small way, being in this business, I felt that I could contribute a bit to other people's dreams and make a difference – not only in my life but to millions of others, just like the contributions made to me by many others from this world of movies who came before me.

Not unlike the child in *Cinema Paradiso*, I grew up loving movies. Living in China and Chile, I first encountered America through the black and white movies of the 1930s and 1940s put out by Hollywood. Those moving images changed my life. They shaped my love for all the values I could get from them: love, romance, the definition of good and evil, history, literature, character story, fantasy and reality. My mother Dora had made clothes for Chinese actresses and my dad had an encyclopedic memory for old movies.

They also colored my views of America and changed my perception of history (which was my field of study at UCLA), as they did my perception of people of all colors, creed, and religion. I believed what I could do was to bring these same dreams to others; a look at the human heart, the humanity in all of us – the light and dark of it.

In 1957 when I first arrived in the United States, after wanting to come to the land of my dreams, I never would have known that I would end up in the business of making films. I entered the film business in 1964 as a mail room clerk at Universal Studios. I spent the next ten years as an agent to such people as Terrence Malick, John Milius, Steven Spielberg, Hal Ashby, Michael Crichton, Philip Kaufman, George Cukor, Robert Aldrich, Tony Richardson, Karel Reisz, Lindsay Anderson, Donald Sutherland, Jane Fonda, Martin Landau, Warren Oates, Jack Palance, Gene Wilder, Peter Boyle, George Sanders, among many others. I never dared to direct, or to be a star, or tried to be an actor – I was probably too shy and afraid of failure.

I have been very lucky. To quote J. G. Ballard's title, who was also incidentally born in Shanghai, these are the "miracles of life." Every dream I've had has come true and along the way, some nightmares too. My dad was 87 when he passed away a couple of years ago – I know he is smiling down on me. As a young boy in China, every move was a dramatic change of life and every change of life was about giving a better life to his family.

Over the years I have been involved with over 315 films, some of which I had more to do with than others. I have made many friends, all of whom contributed greatly to my life. My mentors included Arthur Krim, Eric Pleskow, Bill Bernstein, and the people I have worked with such as Milos Forman, Martin Scorsese, Woody Allen, Blake Edwards, Phil Kaufman, and Hal Ashby, among others.

Well after 45 years, I'm still standing; mind you I'm probably a bit smarter and wiser, not angry, not daunted by challenges, and I'm still trying to make a great film.

Also I'd be remiss if I didn't thank Arnie Messer, who has been my partner for the last 16 years. In addition, Gerry Schwartz for his guidance and friendship and Ron Burkle for believing in me when I started Phoenix.

I'd also like to thank my friends at the Kennedy School – a special mention goes to Joe Nye and David Ellwood – my history professors at UCLA, like Albert Hoxie and Robert Burr. My thanks also go to Richard Haas at the Council on Foreign Relations who was kind enough to give me some advice on this project.

And finally to those people who for the past 15 years have been the center and love of my life: my wife Irena and my children, Nicky and Brian.

Mike Medavoy

# Index